Healing and Liberation of Children through Brief Drama Therapy

Akeyo Onoe introduces a new approach in brief drama therapy for children called Improvisational Drama of Acceptance and Mirroring (IDAM). Developed in Japan, it can be used with children in large groups, making it a time and cost effective therapy tool for therapists to add to their toolkit.

IDAM is effective for practice in schools and communities where many children gather together. A strength of the approach is the use of play acting a scene between the Mother, played by the therapist, and a child. The most significant functions of the therapist are acceptance and mirroring. When a child is deeply accepted by the Mother figure in a drama, even for a few minutes, they absorb this meaningful experience instantly, being liberated from oppression or prohibition and empowered with great joy. The book shows how effectively and profoundly this brief therapy helps children touch on their hidden issues, grow, and heal themselves creatively in a short time. Additionally, the book expounds how this approach can be effectively applied to adults who have attachment trauma from childhood.

This book is the first to present a brief drama therapy approach developed in Asia. Though it focuses on mother-child relations in Japan, it is connected to all cultures in principle, and will help increase readers' cultural competency and humility. The content includes practical applications of IDAM and is a great tool for training therapists.

Akeyo Onoe, RDT/BCT, is a pioneer of drama therapy in Japan, and actively promotes it in clinical settings and for people's appreciation of life. She is a professor at the Graduate School of Human Science of Ritsumeikan University and a lecturer at Tokyo University, and representative of Drama Therapy Education & Research Center in Japan.

AKEYO ONOE

Healing and Liberation of Children through Brief Drama Therapy

Acceptance and Mirroring with the Mother-Figure

Routledge
Taylor & Francis Group
LONDON AND NEW YORK

Cover image credit: Getty images

First published 2026
by Routledge
4 Park Square, Milton Park, Abingdon, Oxon, OX14 4RN

and by Routledge
605 Third Avenue, New York, NY 10158

Routledge is an imprint of the Taylor & Francis Group, an informa business

ISBN: 978-1-032-93246-0 (hbk)
ISBN: 978-1-032-93245-3 (pbk)
ISBN: 978-1-003-56506-2 (ebk)

DOI: 10.4324/9781003565062

Typeset in Joanna
by Apex CoVantage, LLC

To my late mother, Junko Onoe
With gratitude for her creativity, great sense of humor, and her spirit of loving and encouraging people, all of which laid the foundation of my serving people as a drama therapist.

Table of Contents

Acknowledgements

I would like to express my most heartfelt gratitude to all the people who supported and helped me in the publication of this book.

All the children at schools and the clients at an addiction recovery facility whom I have had the privilege of working with are my treasures, and they have served as my wonderful teachers.

Professor Emeritus Sally Bailey at Kansas State University has been my supervisor and mentor ever since I encountered drama therapy, and she will remain to be so. Her professional style and integrity in her work and research have affected me greatly and become my role model as a drama therapist and human being. She reviewed many versions of my manuscript in her busy schedule. Without her thorough and insightful feedback and continued reassuring support, this book would not have been out in the world.

Professor Laura Covault at California State University reviewed the manuscript and gave me a lot of important advice and furthered more steps for this publication. Dr. David Read Johnson at Institute for Developmental Transformations and Professor Nisha Sajnani at New York University, both of whom I respect as drama therapy leaders, also read the manuscript and inspired me brightly. Professor Kaoru Nishimura at International Christian University and the reviewers at Japanese Association for Group Psychotherapy reviewed the original thesis of the first part of Chapter Five and provided many helpful suggestions and warm support. Professors Takeo Miyakawa, Akihiro Odanaka and Hirotaka Nanba also gave me useful comments when I wrote the original Japanese book, upon which this English version of the book is based.

Senior Editor Katie Peace, Editorial Assistant Chelsea Low Yingqi, and Senior Production Editor Natalie Meylan of Routledge professionally supported and completed the publication of my first book in English.

I appreciate the Program for the Promotion of Academic Publications of Ritsumeikan University for providing a grant to cover part of the preliminary translation. Especially Tatsuya Kobayashi in the relevant section supported me very much.

Numerous other people helped create this book, such as schoolteachers and staff at recovery facilities, both of whom cooperated in drama processes, my teachers and colleagues in the field of drama therapy, and friends. All of these people have given me real and moral support. Thus, this book is the result and embodiment of my gratefulness to many, many people.

Last but not least, I sincerely thank you, readers, for taking up this book and reading it. My most humble hope is that this book accompany and assist you in your therapy practice and research, enhancing well-being of children and adults alike.

About the Author

After engaging as an actor and announcer in news and educational programs in Japanese media, Akeyo Onoe was chosen and dispatched as a researcher in 1999 to College of Fine & Applied Arts at University of Illinois in the US under the Program of Overseas Study for Upcoming Artists by Japanese Agency for Cultural Affairs. Then she encountered drama therapy at Kansas State University as if guided by destiny. She became the first RDT and BCT in Japan under North American Drama Therapy Association.

She published two books in Japanese on drama therapy: one for the general public titled *Heart Liberating Drama Therapy* and another on an approach for children, on which this book is based. She also translated *Acting for Real* (by R. Emunah) into Japanese, and recently edited a book on art-based research (ABR) in Japanese.

She maintains that drama therapy should not only be for clinical and educational sites but also be a medium that enhances creativity of many people for their appreciation of life, to which she is determined to commit herself as long as she lives.

She is a professor at Graduate School of Human Science of Ritsumeikan University and a lecturer at the Department of Education of Tokyo University, where she provides courses to enhance self-other cognition, skills of helping profession and creativity through drama therapy, and representative of Drama Therapy Education & Research Center in Japan, which provides drama therapy training.

onoe@hs.ritsumei.ac.jp
dtercen@yahoo.co.jp
http://dtcenter-english.hopto.org/

Foreword

by Sally Bailey, MFA, MSW, RDT/BCT
Professor Emeritus, Former Director of the Drama
Therapy Program at Kansas State University

How does a drama therapist develop a new approach? It obviously can't be done in a week or a month. It requires identifying a therapeutic need for a specific population of clients, followed by idea generation, experimentation, reflection, revision, testing, and replays of that cycle until the kinks have been worked out. This book shares how Akeyo Onoe, RDT/BCT, created Improvisational Drama of Acceptance and Mirroring (IDAM), a drama therapy intervention aimed at the needs of Japanese children.

Before becoming a drama therapist, Akeyo Onoe had a career as an actor and announcer in Japan. She came to the US to study theatre and discovered drama therapy when she attended a weeklong intensive class at Kansas State University. She recognized drama therapy could be a powerful method to help people heal from painful experiences and begin to believe in themselves again. Wanting to bring that kind of healing back home, she started studying drama therapy through the North American Drama Therapy Association's Alternative Training Program.

Akeyo found that some Western drama therapy techniques worked well for Japanese people, but that new types of interventions were needed to address certain cultural issues and mental health needs specific to clients in her country. IDAM was first developed for elementary-aged school children, who are put under great pressure to succeed in school. They are expected to behave themselves perfectly at all times and study, study, study. This pressure comes at them from all directions: school, home, and Japanese culture as a whole.

An IDAM session starts with a series of warm-up games, which prepare students for working together and developing basic improvisational skills. Then Akeyo invites individual volunteers to act out a scene in which she plays a fictional mother and the volunteer plays a fictional child. This provides the student actors an opportunity to speak up for themselves and behave differently from their normal obedient manner. Each scene is kept short, lasting several minutes and follows a four-step scene structure common in Japanese narrative. Response from the classroom audience is always expressed as a release of tension through joyous laughter by the student audience.

As Akeyo repeatedly played out these scenes, she noticed that students quickly learned to improvise and express themselves, get in touch with their creativity, and relax from their stresses. The teachers felt this drama therapy experience made a positive difference in the students' attitudes towards their studies and abilities to focus. They asked her back to work with their students again. They told other teachers, and Akeyo was invited into more classrooms.

Akeyo noticed patterns in the scenes that worked well and discovered that the most successful were those where she carefully mirrored the emotions of the student actor at a slightly lower intensity. This created a feeling of connection or attachment between the fictional child and the fictional mother and gave the student actor a chance to take control at the beginning of the scene. As the scene progressed, Akeyo, using a careful modulation of emotion and reactions to the student actors, was able to guide them to a resolution of the scene that involved the child experiencing total acceptance and validation from their classmates and their fictional mother. The final result was a catharsis that allowed them to release their tension without inciting rebellion in ordinary reality. Following that release, students experienced a sense of agency, learned a way to look at the difficult moments in their everyday lives from a different perspective, and ultimately found themselves able to deal better with frustrating life moments. It often led to better communication and reduced tension at home, without the "inappropriate behavior" expressed in dramatic reality being replayed in ordinary reality.

I believe one of the fundamental change agents in these scenes, besides Akeyo's skillful mirroring and empathy with the child actor, was her ingenious use of the ISO principle in a dramatic setting. The ISO principle has been used in music therapy since the 1940s when developed by Ira Altshuler to assist in modulating mood changes in clients. The client is guided away from a negative mood (sad, angry, tense, or anxious) by listening to a series of musical pieces. The first piece matches their mood, and the next ones guide them step by step to a more positive, open one. Applied to IDAM, the fictional mother (played by the drama therapist) connects with the fictional child where they are at emotionally in the beginning of the scene, then slowly modulates them to a new mood in which they can experience the understanding and unconditional acceptance of *amae* by the end of the scene. *Amae* is the Japanese state of deep attachment and acceptance of a child by their primary caregiver.

As time went on, Akeyo found that some adults also needed this type of experience, too. They had experienced similar educational pressures when they were children that created conflicts that blocked their emotional connection with their mothers. These disconnects seemed to melt away when adult clients were able to experience the same mirroring and connection with a fictional mother in a short IDAM scene, just as children do. Adults reported feeling better able to accept themselves and others, to learn how to parent their children with warmth and *amae*, and grew in their empathetic abilities.

I believe you will find Akeyo's descriptions of IDAM fascinating. Her ability to focus on her scene partners and provide them with unconditional positive regard demonstrates great amounts of empathy expressed through play. She explains not only the observable behavior in the scenes, but also her thoughts and reactions as she performs in the scenes and brings closure to the class with another series of expressive drama games. The healing comes from exaggerated situations played out joyfully and with great respect for the child actor's feelings and frustrations. As you read her careful analyses of her process, you will see how reflection on one's interventions can develop deep, subtle, and accurate therapeutic relationships in a short amount of time.

Much of the writing about drama therapy interventions has come from the West, but drama therapy is an international therapy modality practiced across the globe. Those of us in the West have little knowledge about how drama therapists in other parts of the world help people prevent and intervene with mental health challenges. Akeyo Onoe's IDAM intervention is a preventative intervention meant to release the stress surrounding school pressure before serious depression or other forms of mental illness result.

Introduction

1. A NEW METHOD EMERGES FROM CHILDREN

"Every time, the fun time passed in the blink of an eye. Thanks to this drama therapy, I was able to relieve stress, and I enjoyed myself a lot every time. Please continue to provide a good time to as many people as possible so that people around the world can live every day with a smile." R.O.

This is the impression of a fourth grader at elementary school who participated in my sessions.

As a pioneer in Japan, I have practiced drama therapy in a variety of settings, such as educational, clinical, and business, and have felt confident about its effects. This book aims to disseminate to the world a new approach of brief drama therapy for children, called Improvisational Drama of Acceptance and Mirroring (IDAM) which I created to contribute to the healing, liberation, and growth of children. It will open a new area of drama therapy for children in a larger group, who are not without latent problems in their current family and social lives. I will elucidate IDAM so that readers can practice it and even beginners can understand it.

Bailey (2010) announces, "Art is communication-as simple, and as profound, as that" (p. 15), and Way (1998) asserts that art is a significant factor for children's development "[f]or full and rich living" (p. 6), meaning living with the whole of oneself. Knill (1999) affirms that human beings need nourishment and medicine of the psyche or soul, which are taken as healing by the arts, just like the physical body needs diet.

The impetus for the creation of this approach came from elementary school teachers and principals in Japan who understood the need for the arts and were interested in my drama therapy activities. What inspired me was that when I played the role of a mother in an improvisational drama in the session that I first conducted at an elementary school many

DOI: 10.4324/9781003565062-1

years ago, the children received the drama with so much zest. When they understood that this drama was a place where they can do whatever they want, almost all the children in every class volunteered, saying, "I want to perform!" In a drama, it looked as if what they could not do or say in real life instantly overflowed and manifested itself, as if they had lost all restraint inside them. In such a situation, children *amaeru* on (Japanese term for "to depend on another's love": see Doi's theory in Chapter One) or rebel against the "mother," in their interactions with her. The audience also becomes very excited and cheers for the performers with a big laugh, saying, "Keep going!" Receiving cheers from the audience, the performers are filled with more energy. Children repeat the same kind of scene one by one until the therapist who plays opposite them becomes nearly tired of it, and both of those who seem to have no problems, as well as those who seem to have problems, are all absorbed in this drama. Their enthusiasm was so great that when I said it was time to end, they all booed loudly.

2. THE PURPOSES AND EFFECTS OF IDAM

I have profoundly been aware that drama therapy is necessary and useful for "healthy groups" in terms of prevention, actively promoting mental health and creative enjoyment, while I also deeply understand its effectiveness in clinical settings. The children in this book go to public elementary schools and are considered "typically developing" pupils. However, serious problems, such as school avoidance, social withdrawal, bullying, and suicide, are not uncommon there as well. Under the current circumstances where children around the world are affected by the pandemic and atrocious events, therapists, teachers, and parents are all in search of new ways to reach them as they struggle with depression, anxiety, and lack of morale.

Knowing that it is necessary to approach and transform environments and society as a whole to advocate for children, this book suggests what therapy can contribute as IDAM is one of the effective ways to help children in such situations. The readers will learn how to practice this approach at schools, communities, and institutions where many children gather.

Even children who do not *seem to* have any major problems may have accumulated negative energy due to various stresses. It is necessary to identify and accept stress in children and have them express it as early as possible. When children are given *a free and safe* space through

IDAM, they immediately express feelings that they normally suppress (especially aggressive and negative emotions) and what they cannot say or do directly to others. Although it is needless to say that care and therapy after something goes wrong is important, drama therapy is effective as a preventive measure before problems occur. Slade (1954) notes that one of the most important reasons for conducting drama activities for children at school is not to seek a healing effect, but a more constructive reason: preventing problems from occurring. Although this approach is naturally very useful in clinical settings, I hope that you will understand that IDAM conducted at school has deep significance as you read how these children heal and grow, while enjoying improvisational drama from the bottom of their hearts.

Some students in my graduate school who encounter drama therapy for the first time ask me why performing an improvisational drama in a fictional situation leads to "therapy" and "healing" for clients. The reason is that even if the setting is fictional, *the feelings expressed there are real.* Moreover, because it is a fictional space where players play the role of another person, they gain distance from reality, and they can safely externalize what they cannot directly show or express in real life. Although it seems to be a paradox, this is a basic and important theory of drama therapy and key to its appeal. For instance, if you have the feeling of wanting to bully someone but cannot do so in reality, you can express that feeling as a character in a drama if you are given the role of Cinderella's stepmother.

"[T]here is not a child born anywhere in the world, in any physical or intellectual circumstances or conditions, who cannot do drama" (Way, 1998, p. 3). Children have more imagination and creativity than adults. They have the ability to place themselves in the world of drama and "heal" much more easily and quickly than adults. When I accept all the raw emotions of a child directed at me in an improvisational drama, living truthfully in the moment with the child, even for a very short time, this helps them gain emotional balance, heal their heart, and relieve stress. Sometimes violence is sublimated, therefore possibly reducing the acting out of violence in real life. In this process, it is often seen that children (unconsciously) change and expand their perspective of how to accept and feel the cause of their problem. At the same time, IDAM brings children a feeling of satisfaction, success, and catharsis (purification of emotions) and, as a result, improves their self-esteem. Moreover, IDAM brings group transformations with multi-layered effects, which enable them to get along with each other and enjoy going to school more, as well as enhance their creativity, expression, and presentation.

To put it simply, IDAM, with the therapist playing opposite a child, is a place of *a few-minute mutual interaction in which they exert all their powers to accept anything that comes out of the child and reflect the child's world like a mirror in the protected framework of drama*. The most important point is that it be also an enjoyable drama and not fall into a serious atmosphere for a child, while group members are watching. The negative feelings of a child do not belong only to themself but are shared by the audience. This may be one of the reasons why children feel refreshed and good through IDAM. "[D]rama as therapy sets a stage in which truths are revealed, deeper levels of communication and understanding are attained, and the personal reverberates toward the universal" (Emunah, 2020, p. 35).

3. FEATURES OF THIS BOOK AND THE UNIQUENESS OF IDAM

1. The book aims to help promote cultural competency and humility

The book describes a unique approach developed from the drama therapy practices with children in Japan.

Practices and research of drama therapy have so far mostly developed on the basis of cultures and societies of the Western hemisphere. Recently, however, the World Alliance of Dramatherapy was founded and the whole of drama therapy community has started to transform drama therapy to be a field that will apply to many more cultures and be open to multiple cultures truthfully. Further, the North American Drama Therapy Association (NADTA) has also created the Cultural Humility, Equity and Diversity (CHED) Committee to promote this area (NADTA, 2021). NADTA requires Registered Drama Therapists and Board-Certified Trainers to take 15 out of 30 units on this theme in Continuing Education in order to renew their qualification. This tendency is expanding to all fields of therapy.

In line with this, the book will help therapists from English-speaking countries when they are working with clients who come from Asia and still have strong cultural ties. There are to date no books on drama therapy in Japan available in English; in fact, there are no books on Asian drama therapy approaches in English. Readers will learn about the separation from, and common ground with, the mother-child relations in Japan, which will enrich their attitudes toward children and adults in different cultures.

2. Intensive illustration of IDAM on the theme of Mother-Child

IDAM touches on a unique mother-figure in Japan (Asia) and explores the world of children. "The mother" in the context of this book can be interpreted as anyone who is a primary caregiver of the child who will nurture and love them, but nevertheless also controls and suppresses them. It could be other than a mother, such as a father, a grandmother, or so on, in the case of a child with an absent mother. The main activity of IDAM is a drama between a mother/primary caregiver (played by the therapist) and a child. The most significant functions of the therapist are, just like an authentic mother, acceptance and mirroring. When a child is deeply accepted by the mother in a drama, even for a few minutes, they absorb this meaningful experience instantly, being liberated from oppression or prohibition and empowered with great joy. For one moment, they experience a "life of contentment."

While IDAM has the aim of actively promoting the mental health of children in general, it is also very useful for traumatized children in clinical settings. For instance, IDAM was effective in a long-term therapy that I provided for abused children at an orphanage.

3. A shorter time, more children, and a good result

IDAM is very brief as a group therapy, as short as three (or fewer) sessions of around 90 minutes for a group of up to as many as 30 or 40 children. The dramatic space has a specific structure. The session mainly consists of short, continuous, one-on-one therapeutic improvisational dramas between the therapist in the role of a mother and one child, under the fullest care by the therapist, with all the other children observing the drama as an audience. This structure inspires and engages deeply both an acting child and the other children just watching. Each drama is only a few minute long, and each volunteering child plays a drama only once within the whole process. Yet, this short drama can make a big difference in the child. For this reason, I have decided to call IDAM "super brief drama therapy." The term "brief" here means not only a few sessions, but also a child's instant and deep immersion into the drama and immediate liberation thereafter. The book shows how well and profoundly it helps children grow and heal themselves creatively in such a short time.

Although therapy can be provided in schools and various other facilities, it is usually not possible to offer therapy to every single child there. Thus, it is quite time and cost effective.

While this approach is presented as a series of a few sessions for a group of many children, it will work in the same way for a small number of children or for a series of many sessions. If you can afford a therapist on a long-term basis, you can implement IDAM into a much longer program over an extended period. It will also become a tool to assess who needs further or more specified therapy.

4. You can journey with the therapist

Another feature of this book is that you can make a journey to understand children by re-experiencing the fascinating world of drama with each child from the same perspective as the therapist. All the case descriptions present the procession of each drama and reflection by the therapist together with a lively and multi-layered depiction of a child's behavior outside of the drama and movements by the teacher and the other children in the group, which gives a very vivid and truthful picture of each dramatic scene. I hope that the readers resonate with the children's genuineness, pain, emotional changes, and liberation. As the readers can gain from the book a meta-level understanding of IDAM processes, they will attain practical knowledge about how IDAM works in a group. In addition, many impressions and letters from children are presented to show the effectiveness from the perspectives of therapy recipients.

5. Application to adults

Since its publication in Japanese, this book has been well received as a textbook for courses dealing with drama therapy, which are offered at both undergraduate and graduate schools. I have added to the English version of this book one new chapter on applying IDAM to adults with two additional purposes: for adult clients who did not receive sufficient care from their mothers/caregivers when they were children and for training drama therapists. Furthermore, it can also be utilized for healing and as parent training for mothers/parents. Accordingly, this book is also beneficial for therapists for populations other than children.

4. POOP IN THE PANTS!

The first case that I would like to introduce is one in which a child unconsciously tackled his current problem and seemed to have healed himself.

A, a nine-year-old boy, had started to defecate in his pants even at school. His homeroom teacher said that this might be due to a mother-child relationship problem. I heard that his mother had to spend all her energy caring for his younger sister and that her psychological state was not stable. This child-rearing distress is particular to mothers in Japan (Kashiwagi, 2015), who are bound by the norm of motherhood (Inoue, 2013), although it may appear as equitable conflicts between a more independent primary caregiver and a child in other cultures. Actually, in IDAM, where I played the role of his mother, he rebelled against me and clearly said, "I want to annoy Mom." So, it was likely that he was dissatisfied with his mother. When implementing drama therapy at elementary schools, I always try to involve all the students in a class. Basically, I do not approach only specific children with a problem individually. However, before the first session, I acquire information in advance on children about whom the homeroom teacher is worried. Although I involve all children in a class, I proceed with a session so that it can be good for the relevant children.

It would not be entirely off the mark to infer that **A** wanted to attract the attention of his mother, who tended to concentrate on his sister, and had caused the problem of "poop in the pants." Even if true, he himself was unconscious of this fact and did not know why he was actually doing this. As a matter of course, he was very concerned about his pooping problem. I was concerned about how uneasy he felt. The homeroom teacher said that when he defecated in his pants during a class, he was told by some girls around him, "**A**, you smell bad!" It was easy to understand that his self-esteem had become low. According to the teacher, he had begun to be violent towards his friends around that time. He may have expressed his anxiety and frustration in such a way. I wanted to help him externalize his concerns in an enjoyable way. It is easy and appropriate to let children externalize their feelings in a natural way through play.

Accordingly, I conducted an "all-participation-type word association game," in which children can freely say what comes into their minds. This is one of the games that I have created for a session with children, in which all children have to say, all at once, what they associate with the word that I say. The rules allow participants to say whatever they think, using not only a word but also an interjection or a sentence. Unlike a word association game in which participants are required to answer one by one, this game requires participants to say what they think all at once, and it does not matter what they say. The purpose of the game is to utter any word at all to externalize their feelings. For instance, when I say the word "summer vacation," children shout like this: "Fun!", "Short!", and "I don't like homework!" Although I never ask children to shout or scream, they always shout out something and are excited together. When I say the word "mother," they often shout things like "I love Mom!", "Scary!", and "Noisy hag!" So if I want to hear who is saying what, I have to approach the relevant child. In the session in this class, I casually moved to where I could hear **A**'s voice and purposely said the word "toilet" while listening attentively to **A**. He clearly shouted "Poop!" He looked really happy. Since everyone shouted without listening to what the others said, it seemed that he was able to shout what he wanted with complete confidence. It is important to let children externalize their feelings within the framework of play. Imagining his situation at home and school, I wondered how much thought was put into the word that he shouted. Through such a game, a child's ability to turn even anxiety and worry into "play" can be brought out. In adult sessions as well, the same process will occur if you make careful preparations and guide the participants accordingly. However, this ability is demonstrated among children much faster and to a greater extent than among adults!

In IDAM on another day, **A** volunteered to perform a drama. He requested a scenario where he visited his friend's house, ate a baked sweet potato served by his friend's mother, and wanted to poop. I thought inwardly that he had come to the core point and said, "That's a good story. Let's try it!" In this approach, it is vitally important to basically accept any story without evaluation, praise the idea and uniqueness of the story, and have the child perform it. The purpose is to have the child gain a feeling of being accepted and satisfied by accepting all aspects of the child, including even their shortcomings.

A ate a baked sweet potato and said hurriedly, "Oh, I want to go to the toilet." I (playing the role of his friend's mother) mirrored his hurried manner and answered, pointing to the toilet, "The toilet is that way." He then ran into the toilet, where he pretended to defecate and flush the water, and came out of the toilet with a big smile, saying, "Yeah, I feel good now."

Although talking about bodies may be less restrictive in Japan than in some other cultures, mention of bodily functions is shunned in Japan as well. The boy in this case was able to talk about them rather freely as a result of possibly his natural inclination and the class atmosphere to permit such mention.

Kawai (1987, p. 62), a Japanese clinical psychologist, who introduced Jungian psychology to Japan, argues that defecating is an act of "discharging what has accumulated in the body" and appears in dreams and children's play, suggesting some meaning. He notes, showing an example in which a child actually defecated after a psychotherapy session, that the child could have been quite refreshed because she was able to release the hard feelings within her with the help of the therapist. Even though **A** did not actually defecate in the drama, the value of his act would be the same as that of actual defecation. The important point in this case is the fact that he was in time to defecate in the toilet in the drama. One of the greatest benefits of drama therapy is that a participant can rehearse a real-time event. In this case, he was able to gain a realistic feeling of success. After performing the drama, he looked very satisfied. It was clear from his appearance that he felt very good by playing out this scene. IDAM usually performs a mother-child drama at the child's home, but this case deviated by his request and used a scene at his friend's home, and I played the mother of his friend. For him, it had a greater impact that he was in time for his toilet when he was out. He really had a refreshed and happy face. It was very significant that he had been able to be bold enough to perform the act of defecation in official class time while being protected by the framework of the drama. Although he had been told by his classmates that he smelled bad, he was praised, in front of them, by someone like a "teacher" about the content of the drama. This was an important point because it helped him restore his self-esteem. In parallel with this, the opportunity for counseling with the child's mother in such a case may produce faster and better results. IDAM will also work well as a parent training or mothers' healing. However, even if we do not have such an opportunity with mothers, we can help children heal their hearts and come alive by continuing these sessions in which they have their stories accepted unconditionally and are able to play their roles happily in front of others.

After IDAM ended, I had time to perform dramas with the homeroom teacher. Children were very pleased and enthusiastic to watch the dramas. Among the stories requested by the children, there was a scene in which two friends fought over a toy. After the drama, I asked, "Does anyone have any comments?" Then **A** raised his hand vigorously and said clearly, "I saw people fighting in the drama and thought that violence should not be used." The teacher and I had not made any clichéd comments about not being rough with one's friends. We just performed the drama. Although he had been very violent toward his friends around that time, he realized himself, by seeing the drama, that violence was not a good solution. He was able to say this probably because he had experienced being accepted in the previous drama.

Unfortunately, this was the last day that I visited this class, and I did not know what happened after that. However, I presume the drama therapy could have represented a step toward improvement of his condition.

Notes

Readers who want to know actual cases and their practices first may read Chapters Three on cases, Four on conflict cases, and Five on cases for adults, before reading Chapters One on theories and Two on processes/methods.

This book uses gender neutral pronouns for a third-person singular personal noun with no gender distinction except for the parts quoted or referenced from the original, which follow the traditional usage of gender pronouns.

Theoretical Discussions Regarding IDAM

One

1. BASICS OF DRAMA THERAPY

1. What is drama therapy?

Drama therapy is one of the creative arts therapies which synthesizes drama, theatre and psychotherapy. It intentionally uses the inherent healing power of theatre/drama in order to treat mental and physical illnesses and promote inner growth. Its formation has been informed by various fields, some of which are humanistic psychology, psychodynamic psychotherapy, cognitive-behavioral therapy, analytical psychology, psychodrama, play therapy, improvisational theatre in the US, drama education in Britain, and acting theories, such as the one by Stanislavsky (Emunah, 2020; Landy, 1994). Emunah (2020) notes that the objectives of drama therapy are the expression and containment of emotion, developing the observing self, expansion of role repertoire and self-image, and the enhancement of interrelational skills (pp. 22–24). These objectives can be said to be the effects of the therapy.

Drama therapy can be applied in various fields, including medical care, welfare, education, and business, for the purposes of therapy, training, and recreation. Anyone, with or without illness, and from children to the elderly, can improve their quality of life through drama therapy while enjoying it at the same time. It includes a wide variety of approaches, part of which are shown as slices of Bailey's "Drama Therapy Pie" (Dickinson & Bailey, 2024, p. 34). To give some examples, there are fictional approaches such as drama games, non-fictional ones such as Narradrama, process-oriented ones such as Role Method, and presentational ones such as puppetry. Sessions are constituted depending on the population and purpose. IDAM is a fictional approach using improvisation, and while it is process-oriented, it is also presentational as many participants watch the dramas as audience. Drama therapists are usually trained in acting as one of the prerequisites for becoming a registered drama therapist under the North American Drama Therapy Association

DOI: 10.4324/9781003565062-2

(NADTA). Therefore, in some approaches, including IDAM, sessions are facilitated by the therapists acting together with clients.

2. Play, dramatic play, and drama therapy

"Play serves as the stepping-off place for the creative process; all of the arts are forms of play" (Huizinga, 1950 as cited in Bailey, 2010, p. 26). Play is a major element in adult sessions, and it goes without saying that it is essential for children. "Dramatherapy is rooted in play and play is a child's most natural and accessible form of communication" (Bouzoukiz, 2001, p. 21). Play, creativity, and healing are inextricably linked with each other to support children's lives. In particular, pretend play, such as playing house, is a prototype of drama therapy because participants express their true feelings while playing the role of another person who is not themselves. Emunah (2020) notes that drama therapy developed out of "an examination of what Erikson (1940) refers to as the 'autotherapeutic' nature of children's dramatic play" (p. 27).

3. Dramatic play as a therapy

When counselors conducted drama activities with children after the Great Hanshin-Awaji Earthquake in Japan in 1995, children played earthquake scenes many times. They regained mental calm by playing a scene in which they rescued people who were buried under collapsed houses made of cardboard boxes (Fujimori, 1999). It is evident that they fulfilled their desire to have their loved ones rescued in a drama and, as a result, their hearts may have been healed even a little. In addition, their unpleasant emotions may have diminished somewhat by playing a scene of an earthquake many times, where they expressed and spilled out their painful feelings and uncomfortable memories. Just like these plays about an earthquake, which is not an everyday event, children often fulfill their desires and heal themselves through dramatic play in their daily lives.

McCaslin (1984) introduces some views about play as follows:

> Freud's explanation of play as the projection of wishes and the reenactment of conflicts in order to master them is a theory held by many drama therapists . . . Both Eric Erikson and Bruno Bettelheim concurred with this theory, arguing that in externalizing problems and pressures, the player is able to control them. In play an unpleasant experience can be resolved, an enemy beaten, or a problem satisfactorily

solved and put to rest. Witness children "playing school" and exorcising a bad experience through repetition of it in play or a reversal of roles, sometimes collapsing in laughter at the outcome. The unpleasant situation is weakened by playing it. (p. 44)

4. Dramatic reality, distancing, and art as therapy

Pendzik (2006) proclaims the importance of "dramatic reality" as "a core concept in drama therapy" (p. 271). Contrasting with ordinary reality, she explains as follows: "Dramatic reality is imagination manifested . . . [it] involves a departure from ordinary life into a world that is both actual and hypothetical: it is the establishment of a world within the world" (p. 272). It becomes "a safe space into which personal feelings, ideas, relationships, and experiences can be projected" (Dickinson & Bailey, 2024, p. 22), since it is "an imaginary realm, engaging in make-believe play" (Pendzik, 2006, p. 271), being distanced from reality. Also, "distancing is a central concept and tool" (Landy, 1996, p. 14) in drama therapy. One of the major reasons why IDAM works well for children is that they can project their issues creatively at a safe distance in dramatic reality, with a *safe mother* (not with a mother played by other children). "Usually [projection] is an unconscious process" (Jones, 2007, p. 137). While projection is often viewed as a defense mechanism in traditional psychology, Jones (2007) states that "projection is often the inspiration for creative activity" (p. 137). Silverman (2020) also proclaims that "[c]reative projection offers a unique opportunity to simultaneously establish a strong emotional engagement and a safe emotional distance" (p. 33).

While the same processes adults experience should be taking place with children as well, they are less able than adults to verbalize and conceptualize what transpires in their mind during drama therapy, and only express that it was "fun" to play a drama which they create with a "mother." The essence of fun also comes from the setting of a drama being fiction. McNiff (2018) explains that "[r]ather than compromising experience and reality, [fiction] may optimally heighten them" (p. 30). Some of the merits of fiction are, he also states, that you can exert imagination without limitations that exist when interacting with real people, get freedom to enlarge and integrate experiences with others, and access the truth with safety and intensity for all the more reason that the setting is fictional. Landy (1996) says that catharsis occurs at the mean point where one can think and feel, not overflooded with feeling, which is the "aesthetic distance" (Scheff, 1979), where "the possibilities for insight and for psychic healing are very great indeed" (Landy, 1996, p. 27). Children probably meant to say that they were at this point when they expressed their having fun and being refreshed. Children, who have complaints with their own mothers, may be inspired by IDAM to think of relations with their own mothers, but are also engulfed with comfortable feelings of enjoying fiction as well as of being accepted here and now, which can be said that IDAM has given them a mean point from both ends. Another key factor is the comfortableness to be a different person. In a brain study that was done on actors when they act as characters (not themselves), Brown et al. (2019) concluded that "changes in embodiment can lead to neural changes in networks associated with perspective taking and role change" (p. 18). Concretely speaking, when actors are in the roles of Romeo or Juliet, deactivations occurred in the prefrontal cortex, an area of the brain associated with self-awareness. The fact that many children say they feel refreshed after IDAM shows that they can leave their usual selves and enjoy different selves in the drama.

Above is also related to the difference between "art psychotherapy" and "art as therapy." The former approach focuses on psychotherapeutic structures and insights pertaining to relations with the therapist, and the latter considers the art making process itself as the origin of healing and focuses on art making and expression. The purpose of therapy and the situation of a client principally decide which approach to use (Ono, 2011). Drama therapy functions as "art as therapy" or "art psychotherapy" depending on the materials for drama and the ways of facilitation. For instance, playing a fairy tale may usually work as the former. Yet, it will seamlessly change to be "art psychotherapy" if the therapist promotes reflection in connection with the client's real life. IDAM has the two types synthesized. Children enjoy a drama as "art as therapy" in a fictional setting with a proper distance and, unlike psychodrama, they do not play their real home events or their real self. So do the audience children. Despite this setting, due to a realistic scene which I play as a mother, like a scene when a child goes to school in the morning, children are more likely to reflect on their "reality." This very subtle setting of combining both distances renders a play capacity to create the aesthetic distance for children. IDAM is "art as therapy" outside and "art psychotherapy" inside.

5. Differences between drama therapy and general drama teaching

As mentioned above, IDAM is an approach of drama therapy whose main purpose is to let children feel free and relaxed to release their feelings so that they will know the joy of expressing themselves and relieve stress. Accordingly, the approach is different from general drama making and general drama teaching aimed at performing in front of an audience. Since *the process of performing a drama* has significance, emphasis is not placed on whether or not the drama is performed well. Interestingly, however, children who enjoy performing a drama freely without being evaluated eventually become better actors in many cases. Thus, with a focus on the process, children are allowed to perform an improvisational drama freely and to play only the role that they want voluntarily. Consequently, children feel no psychological burden.

Among people practicing drama improvisation, there is a rule called "*Yes and* . . . which requires that whatever 'offer' one actor makes, the other must accept ("Yes,") and add on to ("and . . .")" (Dickinson & Bailey, 2024, p. 36). Also, Takao (2006) states the importance of saying yes to one's opposite, introducing mottos of Johnstone (1979) to give the partner a good time. This concept applies for IDAM. Thus, the therapist playing opposite a child guides them to feel good. This setting is one big difference between IDAM and general drama making/teaching.

The same effect as drama therapy may be eventually obtained through general drama activities (using dramas with a script and lines that players practice repeatedly to perform in front of an audience). In addition, there are many other things that can be learned from general drama activities as follows: speaking words clearly, correctly memorizing lines and movements, and cooperating with others to perform a drama as discussed and practiced from a physical perspective and understanding the feelings of the characters in a drama, and comprehending the subject of a story from the perspective of psychological learning.

However, in a general drama with casting aimed at being performed in front of an audience, some children may have to play a role that they do not want to play and say lines that they do not want to say, cannot play a role that they want to play, or cannot perform well no matter how much they practice. In such cases, instead of feeling refreshed by expressing their feelings, the child may feel miserable or sometimes hurt mentally. As a matter of course, some children in a general drama may feel good when receiving applause from the audience. However, there is a great difference between children who win a good role and those who are given an unwanted role, and between those who play the leading role and those who play the role of a passerby. Moreover, there are some children who feel burdened by being given a major role or a role with many lines. It is very difficult to prepare a script and determine the cast with due consideration to all children, taking into account all such details. McCaslin (1984) notes that most educators since the 1920s have had the view that children under the age of 10–11 should not perform for an audience. The reasons she gives are as follows:

> 1) Teachers who focus on pleasing an audience for the purpose of performing a drama in public tend to impose their thoughts on children when teaching or to always give major roles to good performers and give other children the roles of minor characters and townspeople, or no role at all. 2) The audience (parents) praises only those who act well, and laugh when a performer makes a mistake or does something at the wrong time.

These are not the only reasons. If we prioritize good performances, bottling up children's feelings and forcibly eliciting feelings that they do not really have, this could pose a psychological danger to children. Since "acting" is an act that has a realistic impact on a performer, it is a double-edged sword that brings both positive and negative effects and risks. This might be forgotten if we pay attention only to good performances and the audience.

When I perform IDAM with a child, the audience (classmates) usually enjoys it, and are tempted to perform a drama themselves. When IDAM is viewed only in terms of performance, it might be said that the drama sometimes drags a little and that the audience gets bored if the same sort of thing continues. However, since IDAM prioritizes the feelings of children who perform the drama, it is completely different from dramas that are performed with a focus on the audience.

It is also true that there are cases in which an instructor who is not a drama therapist conducts drama activities to perform a general drama (with a script and an audience) and this goes well (in terms of the fact that children enjoy it, feel good, and grow mentally). It all depends on the attitude, purpose, and method of the instructor. This can only happen when a drama is performed based on a script selected properly under the supervision of a thoughtful instructor. This is also possible when an instructor guides all participants to become single-minded to advance the process of creating a drama and producing the results, for instance, by providing children who do not want a role or who are not given a role with the opportunity to actively work behind the scenes. Under these conditions, I do not deny the positive effects of general dramas with a script aimed at being performed in front of an audience. Even in such cases, however, I believe that use of the approach presented in this book with the process of practicing a drama will help produce better results. Regarding this, McCaslin notes that when the improvisational method is used for a drama with a script, it is recommended to interpret the drama before determining the cast and making players memorize their lines because more focus can be placed on the process of creating a drama than the finished work. She also notes that if a drama can be performed in front of a good audience that appreciates watching a children's drama, it will offer a wonderfully rewarding experience for children.

Although the purpose of the drama therapy approach presented in this book does not primarily include the intention to improve acting coaching techniques and acting skills, use of the approach helps children improve their acting and expressive skills as a by-product in many cases. This is a great satisfaction to me. For instance, I received the following impressions from a child, although I never teach children how to act in the sessions.

> "I have changed after receiving this drama therapy. What has changed is that I have gained acting skills. I performed a drama titled 'Handsome Samurai' at a school fun party. The drama required acting skills, which I learned during the drama therapy. And then, oh my goodness! I can now think that I have become a good performer. I really thank the drama therapy." Y.K.

6. Precautions for improvisational dramas that deal with conflict

Although there are many drama activities, such as drama lessons and workshops, it is important to recognize that without a correct understanding of the true impact of drama, such activities may produce the opposite effect. At one conference, an elementary school teacher talked about a role-play that he conducted in class to teach children that bullying is bad. He cast one child as a bully and another child as a victim in an improvisational drama. In the drama, the child who played the bully picked on the victim viciously. The following day, the child who played the victim was absent from school. When the teacher was asked by the child's mother if something had happened to her child at school, the mother said that he had not stopped hiccupping since he came home the previous day. The teacher realized for the first time that this might have been caused by the previous day's drama. Although the teacher conducted drama activities for educational purposes, thinking that they would be good for the children, they resulted in damaging the child. It might be that the child went home in a state in which he was unable to distinguish reality from the drama while feeling as if he had actually been bullied. I am very sorry that the teacher put the cart before the horse. It seems that he had the false impression that drama would help children learn about bullying at school, without understanding the strong impact of drama. Not only drama therapists but also those who intend to conduct drama-related activities for others should—and indeed have a responsibility to—know this impact of drama. The fact that such knowledge is not widespread is not limited to teachers in general. There are many other people who are not aware of this, even if they are experts in the field of psychology and psychiatry, or even professional actors.

Dramas and plays are embodied forms of art that are very close to real life. To put it briefly, for performers, acting is to live the lives of others, using their body and voice, and feeling the visceral feelings of others and themselves. If they feel positive while acting, this has a therapeutic effect. That is why dramas can serve as a therapy. However, if the performers feel negative while acting, they are damaged or hurt, the same as in real life. Or if they have had a similar negative experience in their real life, they may become re-traumatized. Dramas can have both a positive and negative effect. Based on this recognition, to purposely advance a drama in a good direction, you should not leave an improvisational drama to children only, which can develop in any direction, because you cannot control how it ends. It is even worse when an improvisational drama deals with bullying or other similar themes. That's why the therapist needs to be involved such as playing opposite children, and the children need to be deroled after the scene is over.

It is recommended, as an alternative to playing opposite children, to have multiple therapists/teachers perform a drama in front of the children to have them learn from it. However, it should be discussed as a precondition with the class that there is no real bullying being done and that the drama is performed in a preventive sense.

It is important never to use in a drama setting actual roles or relations of the group in order to deal with actual issues occurring in a group. If bullying exists in a class, where there are both bullies and their victims, they need to be dealt with separately, depending on the seriousness of the problem and the interrelationships within the group in each individual case.

If I use drama to prevent bullying, I do not choose such a direct theme. I will provide repeated opportunities for children to play fun games with drama elements and perform improvisational dramas in which I play opposite a child in order to encourage them to know each other better and to create good relationships with many classmates. I will also try to convey to them in a natural way that every person has different qualities and aspects and that they should enjoy these differences. Consequently, if they can build a relationship of trust with each other in the class, it becomes possible for them to think seriously about bullying even if a fictional drama with the theme of bullying is performed. Use of the drama approach with such an educational purpose produces various by-products and is not limited to preventing bullying.

In addition to the above discourses from perspectives of drama and play, I will next lay out the development of IDAM and its related theories as follows: 1. Accumulation of the author's practices of mirroring; 2. Discourse on mentalization; 3. Discovery and research on mirror neurons; 4. Discourse on mother-child relations.

2. MIRRORING, MENTALIZATION, AND MIRROR NEURONS

1. Why is mirroring effective?

I have offered classes and lectures on communication using drama therapy to a total of tens of thousands of attendees. In these classes and lectures, I have taught that mirroring is a very good technique for creating good relationships with others. In university classes, after basic practice such as a mirroring exercise, in which students do the same movements as the other person, I give them the following assignment and ask them to summarize their results in a report. The assignment goes like this: When they are with someone with whom they want to become friendly in real life, they should mirror their posture, movements, facial expressions, tone of voice, speaking speed, or mood, and if possible mirror the other person's feelings. (When the other person feels sad, they should feel sad together with them before providing comfort, and when the other person is angry about something, they should first get angry with the other person instead of calming them down, etc.) Consequently, a large number of students reported the effects of mirroring with surprise. There were many cases as below:

"After my mirroring my friend, she told me her troubles that she had never talked about before."

"When I listened to what my friend said while mirroring her, she told me that she felt so much better."

"When I listened to what my friend told me while mirroring her, she thanked me very much. Thinking I was able to serve her well, I also felt happy and lively."

As described in the book *Heart Liberating Drama Therapy* (Onoe, 2006), I received reports from other people involved in the service industry who said that they received more words of appreciation and compliments from customers and that their sales increased. As an interesting example, there was a report by an employee who said when he mirrored his superior at work, who had always scolded him, he was scolded less frequently. Another thanked me as she successfully got a position at a new company by using mirroring in her interview. As a miraculous example, when a university student who had spent two years at home, feeling afraid to go to university because she was unable to make friends with anyone, tried mirroring, she gained new friends in three classes. She said that in the future, she would like to tell those who have the same problem that there is a good way to resolve it. In this way, mirroring can make the other person unconsciously experience very positive sensations physically and mentally, and serves as a powerful way to elicit friendliness from them and build a better relationship.

In IDAM, the physical and superficial mirroring of movements and tone of voice only acts as a gateway for sharing the same feelings. This alone is often effective enough, yet, when the therapist further reflects the child's feelings like a mirror and returns them back, the child will come to understand their current feelings. If they have negative feelings, the ultimate goal is to overcome (or transform) such feelings. Mirroring serves as a concrete way to express supreme empathy (when it is done with the right intention and sincerity) and, in other words, as a means of communicating that a therapist accepts the whole person of the other. Examples of the efficacy of mirroring are many as stated above. Yet it is very difficult for teachers and therapists at schools to find occasions to mirror and transform children's emotions, especially negative and strong ones, at the moment they appear, because they do not stay with children

24 hours a day and the number of children in need for such attention will be too many. If they find one, it is hard to exert this practice in a day-to-day situation of reality. Therefore, it is most likely one of the best possible ways to use a "fictional" drama and mirror children in it.

The child resolutely and strongly directs their affection or disobedience to me when I play the role of a specific person (usually a mother) in a drama, all the more for its fictionality. First of all, this seems to be a powerful experience that they have never experienced before. As the mother in the drama, I accept their attitude toward me as it is and share their feelings. While acting the drama, I gradually proceed with the story according to their improvisational reactions. In a short period of time, the child will express (vent) their feelings, have their feelings shared by the therapist in the role, and come to understand the circumstances and changes of their sharing of feelings. There is a high possibility that a child's emotions expressed in a drama are true to their real life, yet the child can express them with ease of mind as they are playing a fictional drama. In addition, their friends are watching it and share the feelings, thus extending the understanding of the feelings even further among the whole group and rendering the whole drama less hurtful to self and others. This enables children to gain a feeling of satisfaction and reassurance and brings a happy ending to their dramas in many cases.

2. Encounter with Fonagy et al.

How is it possible to make all of these experiences happen? What do I do with children in a drama? These were big questions in the early days of my practice. As I searched for theories that may pertain to such effects of mirroring, I found that a British clinical psychologist/psychoanalyst, Peter Fonagy et al. (2002), reported in details clinical surveys and theoretical discourses, which provide a key concept related to the understanding of my practices. While many psychologists and psychotherapists have expounded on either attachment theories or mirroring approaches and concept, Fonagy et al. used a new idea of affect regulation and mentalization to analyze the process of an infant's establishment of the self. Mentalization is the interpretation of the social environment or reconstruction in one's mind of the relations between the world and oneself. The ability to mentalize is the one to imagine the states of mind of one's own and others.

(Note: In order to avoid confusion of interactions between the caregiver and the infant, the following two paragraphs follow Fonagy's usage of pronouns in his book, representing the caregiver as she and the infant – it, instead of gender neutral usage of pronouns.)

Fonagy et al. (2002) argue that when the caregiver mirrors back the infant's affect, the infant receives this affect through the caregiver as if looking in a mirror and the infant recognizes it as its own affect. The caregiver's acceptance of the infant's affect (especially a negative one) thus reflected to her, her modulating it to be a stable and nurturing affect and returning it to the infant enables it to receive the affect as its own with assurance. If, conversely, the caregiver reflects the infant's affect in a much stronger and intensified state, the infant cannot regulate and decouple it from itself. The infant's perception "is likely to escalate rather than regulate the infant's state, leading to traumatization rather than containment" (p. 9). The infant learns affect regulation through an agency of the caregiver who repeatedly accepts its affect in a reassuring and nurturing manner. Fonagy et al. also maintain that the repetition of such "adaptive affect-reflective interaction" (p. 192) between the self and the other leads to the acquisition of mentalization ability, which in turn becomes the basis of promoting the establishment of the self. This ability will be an essential source for a person to understand the other and the world. Therefore, if a person has acquired an insufficient ability of this kind, a treatment will be necessary to enhance and increase it.

They illustrate the interactions of the mother conducting an affect-mirroring with the infant as follows:

When the infant expresses its affect with all its force, there is no separation between the self and the other. It is the state where the infant expresses the affect without limitation. The caregiver (usually its mother) mirrors this affect and accepts it, saying, "Oh, good, it is alright now," and returns it to the infant in a slightly modulated form. The mother assumes the feelings of the infant and, using her own facial and vocal expression, represents these feelings to the infant. Here "markedness" (p. 192) is very important and the mother has to "pretend" in her affect-mirroring. The caregiver at this moment should not throw back her own real emotions that directly respond to the infant's emotions. Also, the caregiver should reassure and calm rather than intensify the infant's emotions. This is a typical affect-mirroring. It is by such affect-mirroring that the caregiver develops affect regulation in the infant. The infant gets the sense of a boundary between self and other, and it comes to accept its own affect as belonging to itself by sensing the image of the caregiver mirroring its internal experience of emotions, that is to say, "a representational framework" (p. 9) is created in the infant because the caregiver reflects its affect.

This is precisely one effect that IDAM intends to achieve. IDAM promotes exactly the process of children stabilizing in their mind and being led to proper development of mentalization as their emotions are mirrored and shared by the therapist in the role of the mother. I learned that I had been unconsciously performing the same process in IDAM in my initial days of using it, intuiting that it was most significant to accept and mirror children's emotions, and then I began to do that intentionally and formulated this approach. The theory by Fonagy et al. clarified the meaning of such processes and let me understand theoretically why children enjoyed this drama so much, felt satisfied, and gained a sense of stability. It also made great sense to me that those children in particular, whom I could imagine from their background seemed to not have received enough mentalizing from their caregivers, often enjoyed much more and sent me letters with more thanks to me.

As explained above that pretending is important, the key to mirroring the child's affect is to conduct it not at the same level of its feelings but at a controlled level with slightly less strength. Since the same affect, if emitted at a stronger level than that of the child, will overwhelm the child and work as a restraint. Mirroring's purpose is to ease the child so they can let out their affect, should be at an expressive level with slightly less capacity. In this approach, I have long felt that I never play the role "seriously" on the surface. I always end up playing with reduced seriousness and controlled acting, sometimes playing in a very unrealistic fashion. This coincides exactly with the argument by Fonagy et al. that says, "the caregiver must somehow indicate that her display is not for real: it is not an indication of how the parent herself feels" (p. 9).

3. From the perspective of the action of mirror neurons

The discovery of mirror neurons asserts that interaction with children through mirroring in IDAM is well verified from the perspective of neuroscience. I would like to briefly expound here about the workings of the mirror neurons that exist in the brains of humans and monkeys (and many other animals), and their implications upon IDAM. I remember being very excited when I found out about them in an article in an American scientific journal. Mirror neurons are nerve cells in the brain that are activated whenever a person performs an action and whenever they witness someone else performing the same action. They were discovered in 1990s by Giacomo Rizzolatti, an Italian neurophysiologist, and his colleagues. These neurons were named mirror neurons as they reflect others' actions within the brain like a mirror, as if they were performing the same actions themselves. V. S. Ramachandran, a neuroscientist in the US, suggests that this discovery is comparable to the discovery of DNA in biology (Iacoboni, 2008, p. 8). One important point is that we can understand the meaning of other people's actions and predict their next action thanks to the existence of these neurons. One of the leading researchers in the US, Marco Iacoboni (2008) declares that the results of some important experiments clearly support "the mirror neuron hypothesis of empathy," i.e., "mirror neuron areas help us understand the emotions of other people by some form of inner imitation" (p. 119). According to the hypothesis, he continues, "our mirror neurons fire when we see others expressing their emotions, as if we were making those facial expressions ourselves. By means of this firing, the neurons also send signals to emotional brain centers in the limbic system to make us feel what other people feel" (p. 119).

Rizzolatti and Sinigaglia (2006) introduce an instance when Peter Brook, an eminent theatre and film director, said that the discovery of mirror neurons led neuroscience to finally begin to understand what has been commonly known in the theatre world, i.e., the fact that the audience participates in a drama actively and shares actors' actions and emotions within themselves. They state that the study of mirror neurons seems to "provide an experimental and theoretical framework for the first time in history" to decipher such workings (p. 11). If applied to IDAM, mirror neurons could be said to make it possible that the therapist understands the child's actions and emotions and, further, the audience understand those of the acting child.

Iacoboni (2008) writes that mirroring is "a powerful mechanism" for understanding the emotions of other people and empathizing with them, and there is a lot of evidence supporting a lot of mirroring between parents and their children. It is interesting to note that the results of an experiment in which mothers watch their own babies suggest that they not only mirror the emotions of the facial expressions of their babies but also simulate the appropriate actions to initiate afterwards, in the brain. He explains that in real life, for example, the mother understands that she has to do an appropriate reaction of comforting her child for an effective interaction, more than just crying together with the baby when it is crying.

He further states how mirror neurons function in recognition of self and others as follows:

> . . . mirror neurons in the infant brain ***are formed by the interactions between self and other***. This is the key concept to keep in mind for understanding the role of mirror neurons in human social behavior. It makes sense that later in life, we use these very same brain cells to understand the mental states of other people. But it also makes sense that we use the same cells to build a sense of self, since these cells originate early in life when other people's behavior is the reflection of our ***own*** behavior. In other people, we see ourselves with mirror neurons (p. 134).

This is precisely a neuroscientific explanation of the theory of Fonagy et al. Iacoboni states, "Babies love to play imitation games," and the specific reciprocal imitation (and chemistry) between parents and babies "may be one of the major shaping factors in reinforcing mirror neurons in the developing brain" (p. 49). In that sense as well, mirroring in IDAM can be said to be valuable, in particular, for children. Mirroring is more necessary for children who were not in a proper and adequate state of mutual imitation with their caregiver when they were an infant.

Iacoboni calls "the mirror neuron research an existentialist neuroscience of sorts" (p. 267) since "the themes raised by mirror neuron research map well onto themes recurrent in existential phenomenology" (p. 266). Introducing that the father of phenomenology, Edmund Husserl, described the phenomenon as "coupling," where we understand others through intersubjectivity, he argues that "the role of mirror neurons in intersubjectivity may be more accurately described as allowing interdependence rather than pure 'coupling'" (p. 265). I interpret his statement on mirror neurons as a confirmation of the interactions happening between children and me in IDAM.

The important keywords for mirroring are "repetition" and "change." In particular, when the therapist firmly accepts the child, their feelings are often expressed many times as the same behavior or attitude. The therapist mirrors and repeats it as well. What is important here is that it is not a real mirror but another person who is doing the mirroring. That is, it is impossible to mirror another person 100% the same way. Precisely because of this slight deviation (or by consciously causing a deviation), the therapist and the child proceed to change themselves through repetition. Buds of these changes become a driving force that helps the drama move to the next step. It is therefore important for the therapist to detect the direction of changes during repetition. Both the therapist and the child change themselves by responding to the changes in the other person. This phenomenon is resonated with what Iacoboni calls "allowing interdependence" when understanding others through intersubjectivity.

3. WHY DOES A MOTHER-CHILD DRAMA HAVE DEEP SIGNIFICANCE?

I would never say that an IDAM therapist should always play the role of a mother, because a mother is not the only person who should look after her child. Depending on the child's situation and wish, it is good for the therapist to play the role of a caregiver other than a mother. Even so, I will discuss why a "mother-child drama" has deep significance based on the fact that in many cases, the mother may be one of the most important people in the world for her child. This also is based on the reaction of children in the mother-child dramas that I have experienced. Although the discussion will be mainly against the background of Japanese culture, the theme of mother-child relations will have a bearing in all cultures in a different way because of the same archetypal properties of mother/primary caregiver.

1. Continued "myth of motherhood"

In 1976, Adrienne Rich published a book that clarified the issues of motherhood as an institution and presented the perspective of the liberation of women. In the same year in Japan, Hayao Kawai, a noted clinical psychologist who introduced Jung to Japan, published the 1976 book titled *Bosei Shakai Nihon no Byori* (*The Pathology of Japan as a Maternal Society*), which spread the understanding that Japan is a maternal society. Coincidentally, a translation of Bowlby's *Attachment and Loss* was issued in Japan in the same year, and its Japanese title was *Boshi Kankei no Riron* (*Theory of Mother-Child Relations*). This indicates that it was taken for granted that it was a mother's duty to raise her children and that even psychologists did not seem to have any doubts about this title (Yamamoto, 2011). At the same time, it was considered that Japan was a society with a high degree of "closeness between a mother and a child" that was unparalleled anywhere in the world, and that this characterized Japanese family relationships, along with the "absence of the father" (e.g., Doi, 2014; Hiraki & Kashiwagi, 2015; Nihonmatsu et al., 2018; Tamura, 1996; Ueno, 2009). As Eva Feder Kittay (1999) proclaimed in *Love's Labor: Essays* in *Women, Equality, and Dependency*, the work of caring for those who depend on others is considered a socially unproductive activity, which has been carried on mainly by women. In Japan an excessive expectation exists for child rearing as a very strong norm for the mother rooted in maternal love (Inoue, 2013).

Time has passed, and the situation in Japan is currently changing, where society promotes the participation and cooperation of fathers in child-rearing. A childcare leave system at birth was established for men in October 2022. However, in order to make this system rooted in society, it is necessary to change the workplace culture and the mindset of men who are obsessed with the idea of the "sexual division of labor" (Nukaga & Fujita, 2022; Tanaka & Ishida, 2022, p. 28). Even if they come home early, husbands, for example, often play smartphone games while their wives are doing housework and engaging in childcare. According to a survey by the Ministry of Internal Affairs and Communications, among dual-income couples with children under the age of six, wives spend more than three times as much time as their husbands on housework and childcare, which is the same result as 15 years ago (Tabuchi, 2022, p. 23). The following survey further shows its background for such disparity. Japanese office workers are strongly biased, at the proportion of one out of three, with the unconscious notion of women for home and men for work, according to a survey of 100,000 people. The survey was based on Implicit Association Test, developed by researchers at Washington University and modified for Japanese (Nakayama, 2024, p. 4). Another survey by the Ministry of Health, Labor and Welfare shows that 60% of women whose husband was unhelpful after the birth of a child and who essentially became a single-parent, divorced when children were younger than five years old ("Husband working . . .," *Asahi Shimbun*, 4-1-2024, p. 17). The international comparison and data in these surveys and media confirm the basis for the phenomenon of the mother's child-rearing anxiety particular to Japan (Kashiwagi, 2015, p. 64). Moreover, according to the World Economic Forum's *The Global Gender Gap Report* 2024, Japan ranks 118th out of 146 countries in terms of the social status of women, which is the lowest level among developed countries, lower even than South Korea, China, and other ASEAN countries. In 2024, Japan was issued recommendations by UN's CEDAW (Committee on the Elimination of Discrimination against Women) to take measures for improvement in wide areas, such as to revise the Civil Code requiring married couples to use the same surname, to eradicate violence on women, and to ensure equality in employment. These recommendations are regarded as "profoundly surprising in light of Japan being a modern state with a huge economy." While the Republic of Korea also in East Asia has improved situations in accordance with the former recommendations, Japan has shown no great progress (Think Gender, 2024, p. 2).

As can be seen from these facts, there is a close relationship between the low social status of women and the need for women to take on the main burden of childcare duties. Although the circumstances surrounding motherhood and child-rearing have become more diverse, a greater burden on working mothers and a mother-child adhesion without a father are still manifested (Nukaga & Fujita, 2022). The myth of motherhood which Badinter (1982) asserts as a social construct and not innate, or maternity belief (Ohinata, 1988) have not receded, and the mother-centered nature of child-rearing still exists.

Update on women's position in Japan

Signifying in October 2025 a historical advent of the first female premier in Japan's history, Prime Minister Takaichi holds conservative positions in gender issues, arousing antagonistic hope and doubt for furthering gender equality through this appointment.

2. Parent and child relationships in Japan and *"amae"*

One publication that raised objection to the mother-centered tradition is the 2017 book, *Regretting Motherhood*, published by Orna Donath, an Israeli social activist, and translated into many languages. She says in her book, "'Women mother'. These two words succinctly describe what has been perceived as a transcultural fact since the dawn of human history: women not only are the main caregivers of their children but are also mothers in themselves" (2017, p. 1). It is significant in itself that some mothers courageously started to openly express regrets and conflicts of being a mother. This book is being read by many in the world. The book was translated in Japan in 2022, and its disclosure of mother's regret, up until then regarded as non-existent, had a great impact in Japan. It gathered the public's attention, and the media reported the voices of mothers who agreed with what Donath advocated. A female reporter in her thirties and the female director of NHK, Japan's public broadcasting corporation, who created a television special, wrote the book, "*If Only I Can Say I Regret Being a Mother: Japanese Women Start Telling*," in which they conducted intensive interviews and found mothers who reported a sense of loss of self-existence and a sense of guilt at not being the "ideal mother" (Takahashi & Yoda, 2024). While the direction is much welcomed that mothers have started to vent their resistance against being looked at as a primary caregiver by society, Donath's widely read book, and its aftermath in Japan, professes how persistent and powerful the myth of motherhood remains and that the mother's influence on her children is itself something singular.

There is a unique, common tendency in how children enjoy acting out IDAM. I can feel a great sense of liberation in them and the moment when they grow up through the drama. What makes me aware of the background to this is the understanding that children are placed in a double-bind situation by their mother, explained by the prominent Japanese philosopher Yujiro Nakamura (1983), the maternal principle and paternal principle indicated by Kawai (1976), and the understanding of the concept of "*amae*" by the eminent Japanese psychoanalyst and psychiatrist, Takeo Doi (e.g., Doi, 1961, 1971, 1981, 1997, 2005, 2007, 2009, 2014). *Amaeru*, a Japanese intransitive verb, cannot be translated into a single English word. It means "to depend and presume upon another's love or bask in another's indulgence." *Amae* is the noun form of *amaeru*. It has the same root as the word *amai*, an adjective meaning "sweet." "Thus *amae* can suggest something sweet and desirable" (Doi, 2005, p. 140). Doi's best-selling book in the 1970s, *Amae no kozo* (English title: *The Anatomy of Dependence*), was highly acclaimed overseas (Yamatake, 2018).

Referring to Bateson's double-bind theory (1972) and Neumann's great mother archetype (1974), Nakamura (1983) argues that even a well-meaning mother has characters of both a mother who protects her children and a mother who tries to control and contain her children for subjugation, and that children are trapped in a state where they cannot separate from their mother to become independent.

Kawai (1976) claims that Japan is a maternal society in comparison with societies of Europe and the US where the logic of "individual" has developed. He sees the maternal principle as acceptance and dependence, and the paternal principle as separation and independence, and he describes that the process of a child's growth is a transition of his foundation from the maternal principle to the paternal principle, where various conflicts arise between the mother, father, and child.

Doi (e.g., 1961, 1971,1981, 1997, 2005, 2007, 2009, 2014) interprets Japanese society as having a structure of *amae*, the basis of which lies in the peculiarity and importance of an intimate relationship between two people such as child and mother/caregiver, friends, husband and wife, teacher and student, employer and employee. He explains that *amae* is the dependency needs of those who wish to be loved by the other person, seeking love passively rather than loving actively, which is the same as Michael Balint's "passive object love" (Balint, 1965, 1968). Balint also refers to this in his book, *The Basic Fault*, and highly appreciates Doi's theory of *amae*. Balint coined the technical term "passive object love" writing, "All European languages are so poor that they cannot distinguish between the two kinds of object-love, active and passive" (1965, p. 56). According to Doi, the archetype of *amae* lies in the infant's search for mother. This is a relationship that allows and encourages the process of the child's ego becoming independent, which is, in fact, not a phenomenon unique to Japan but a common process throughout the world. Doi sees that while people cannot "be their own person" without having enough experience of *amae*, the foundation for accepting such *amae* seems to be becoming lost in recent years.

From the arguments of these three experts, it is understood that it is essential that children are fully accepted and that it is and must be normal for children to have a conflicting relationship with their parent (mother) during the growth process. That is, it can be said that since children grow up while being nurtured, and this itself is a process that contains the contradiction between encompassment and separation/independence, every child is in a state where various conflicts are transforming them from within. They need *amae*/acceptance or separation/independence according to the circumstances of the moment.

3. Excessive burden on Japanese children

If the relationship between the child and the mother seems to be an ideal relationship, free from any conflicts, that could actually be a problem in itself (Nishimura, 2022). Mothers who seem to understand everything about their children and are devoted to taking care of them have a high degree of closeness to their children and are often overprotective and over-possessive of them (Tanaka, 2004). Some children work hard and struggle to meet the excessive expectations of such parents (Makino et al., 2010).

Much worse cases are the presence of many children under mal-treatment in the name of education. They are rid of the will to resist as they are fettered by parents since early childhood. Some children somehow manage to survive by running away from home or turning to delinquency. A well-known incident in Japan took place in 1980 in which a son battered his father to death with a metal baseball bat (Ishii, 2023). In another incident much discussed in recent years in Japan, a daughter stabbed her mother to death in 2018. She was forced by her mother to enter a medical department of a national university, failed for nine years, and finally became a nurse (Saito, 2022). In 2023, another incident took place where a son caught in a similar situation killed both his parents.

The term *educational maltreatment* has started appearing recently in Japan. Its narrow definition refers to parents' enforcement or coercion of education including sports and music upon children that exceeds the limit of their bearing of mind and body, which, together with educational neglect, consists of its broader definition (Takeda, 2021). In the context of this book, I refer to the former definition. Needless to say, society influences this issue greatly, and parents alone are not to be held responsible. Japan has the term *examination war* denoting the fierce competition of entrance examinations, which can be similar to, but may not yet be an act of, maltreatment. As the words illustrate, children are encouraged to compete to get higher marks in examinations and are selected based on examination points for which schools they can enter. Entrance exams for junior high schools are increasing in number, driving parents and teachers to prompt younger children to get as higher points as possible, even by one point (Ishii, 2023). AC Japan is a non-governmental organization that engages in corporate social responsibility and broadcasts messages beneficial to society through advertisements on various media. It even broadcast a Public Service Announcement on television that recommends that children not be immersed in school studies only, but be given due respect as a person (AC Japan, 2024). According to the UNICEF Report Card 16 in 2020, Japan ranks first in physical health but 37th in mental well-being among 38 countries (in OECD or EU). The result is "paradoxical" (UNICEF-The State of the World's Children 2024 Statistical Compendium: Japan). Also, since 1998, the UN's Committee on the Rights of the Child has continued to issue Japan a number of concerns and recommendations. Its latest recommendations in 2019 points out the situation of children being in "stressful school environments, including an overly competitive system" and "their childhood and development being harmed by the competitive nature of society." It also confirms that it is "health issues particular to Japan as well as parts of East Asia to overcome these situations which exert health damage upon children's 'life,' 'protection' and 'development'" (Noi, 2021). Japan and the Republic of Korea are pointed out that both their educational systems and societies are competitive, yet they are the only countries in OECD which ratified the Convention on the Rights of the Child.

The number of suicides of Japanese as a whole decreased in 2024, yet suicides of children in elementary, junior, and senior high schools reached a record high. The most given reasons or motives are "school issues," such as poor performance at school, trouble through the school path, or conflicts with friends (Kawano, 2025). Also, the number of violent behaviors by children was the highest in 2023, and included quite an outstanding number of elementary school students. It is conjectured that pupils' inability to express their feelings may lead to acting out (Honma, 2024, p. 19).

Women's low position and pressure on children in Japanese society delineated above should develop noticeable phenomena where mothers have a high degree of codependency or closeness to their children, enough to spoil them, and where conflict between them becomes bigger due to an oppressive/dominant relationship with excessive expectation on children from the mother representing both parents. It is easy to see that these two phenomena may appear contradictory but are actually two sides of the same coin. These relationships make it difficult for children to rebel, oppose the mother, feel that they are respected and accepted as individuals, and acquire a sense of freedom and independence of mind.

In literature, for example, the bestselling novel, *Where the Crawdads Sing* (Owens, 2019), describes that Kya, still a small child, longs for her mother to return at any moment, despite her strong resentment and revolt against her mother for deserting her. Proust's classic, *The Remembrance of Things Past* (1983), depicts in the beginning that "I," a small child, waits impatiently for "my" mother to come to his room, harboring jealousy and expectant feelings for his mother who forgot a good-night kiss due to her attention to party guests.

If these two children were to play freely a drama of their own choice with the mother (played by the therapist), what drama would they play? How would they play it? If they could express their feelings of anger, control, indulgence, or *amae* without restraint that exists in their real life, they would be able to gain a great deal of catharsis. Beyond the difference of state, culture, age, wealth or poverty, and abuse, children's feelings toward "Mother" should be common, and IDAM will be meaningful for children with good enough efficacy.

4. Attachment and "*amae*"

Doi (1997, 2009) introduced how teachers at a nursery school in Japan discipline children and described their behavior as similar to Bion's

(1959) concept of containment. Their disciplinary approach is "to accept and contain children, which is essentially different from spoiling them. In fact, however, children can *amaeru* only by being treated in such a way. Conversely, when they are spoiled, they, so to speak, lose the initiative and become rather unable to spontaneously *amaeru*" (Doi, 1997, p. 186).

In the discussion so far, some of you may be wondering how Doi's concept of *amae* is different from Bowlby's concept of attachment. Doi recognizes that attachment obviously covers the same area as *amae*. He explains:

> As is known, Bowlby sharply distinguishes attachment from dependence . . . he prefers attachment to dependence as a term, as the former can be more precise than the latter in describing behavior . . . Even so, it seems to me that he overlooks the fact that attachment involves a dependence of its own, as one necessarily becomes dependent on the object as far as one is attached to it. In this regard *amae* definitely has an advantage over attachment precisely because it implies a psychological dependence in the sense mentioned above and unlike attachment refers to the feeling experienced rather than to behavior. All in all, one can say, paradoxical as it may sound, that the concept of *amae* makes it possible to discuss what is not verbalized in ordinary communication, hence is something that remains totally unnoticed if you are speaking European languages. (2005, p. 142)

Also, Kobayashi (2012, 2019), a Japanese psychiatrist and clinical psychologist, claims that there is a great difference between these two concepts. Kobayashi states that attachment is a concept that Bowlby originally brought to psychology from ethology, which is completely contrary to the approach of trying to capture the movement of the mind. Citing Kujiraoka (2012), Kobayashi explains that the concept of attachment focuses on the behavior of whether to approach the other or not and abstracts the area of subjectivity and intersubjectivity, which should be emphasized most in addressing the problem of the mind. Kobayashi provides therapy in which he thoroughly observes the relationship between the mother and the child, not from the perspective of whether the child physically clings to or follows the mother, to decipher the delicate movement of their minds occurring there. For a parent who cannot let the child *amaeru* and a child who is sulky because they cannot *amaeru* despite the desire to do so, he communicates the child's feelings to the mother to endow her with the power of mentalizing. With such therapy, he has produced good results.

Furthermore, according to Endo (2012), the theory of attachment developed as a concept that measures the degree of physical proximity. Later it has come to be used to measure human relationships in adults, which has led to the application of the concept of attachment to representative proximity. He sees that in this context, the distinction between attachment, which is originally intended to avoid a crisis situation and approach in pursuit of affection, becomes ambiguous, and that attachment overlaps with the duality of *amae*, that is, the act of approaching on the premise of affection and the act of seeking affection. In relation to children's growth, he assumes one of the functions of *amae* as follows:

> When the caregiver endures the "*amae*" of a child that is an act of confirming or testing its certainty and accepts it as much as possible, the child may be able to consolidate his conviction in representative proximity and, with this as a basis, gradually acquire true autonomy. (2012, p. 305)

5. Significance of IDAM

When I look at the reaction of a child while playing the role of a mother in IDAM, I can see the mother-child relationship in which the child is placed without meeting their mother. As a matter of course, if there is a therapeutic framework for communicating what the therapist has felt in the drama to the mother in real life, it would be advised to do so. However, even if the therapist does not have the opportunity to see the mother in real life, IDAM can provide a child with liberation and transformation. What is more, this is possible for many children in a short time.

No mother can raise children while accepting everything about them. Therein lies the significance of IDAM. Children can experience appropriate mirroring and mentalizing processes, have the experience of being comfortably accepted and contained by the mother, and freely express themselves in IDAM. Since IDAM is not based in reality, but is fictional, it becomes a place where children can feel both *amae* (containment) and rebellion (independence) to the fullest. They can vent these feelings at the mother, and also enjoy themselves, which seems to provide many children with the experience of "living a satisfactory life (Doi, 1971)" that they have never had before. This is exactly the liberation and growth necessary for them.

The roles played by children can be said to represent natural human tendencies, if not archetypes, such as assertion, rebellion, independence, dominance, escape, liberation, kindness, and coexistence. Kawai (1976) states that "what archetypes manifest in human consciousness is archetypal representation, and when humans experience it, they have vivid and intense feelings." (p. 208). This means even a short, one-time drama can have a great impact on the sensibilities and feelings of children and can be a turning point for them. Even if this happens in a one-on-one relationship with the therapist behind closed doors, it has great significance. Still more in IDAM, it is of enormous significance that this happens in an enjoyable drama in which children's creativity is unleashed in front of classmates who support and witness them. Although children do not understand that such an in-depth process is taking place in a drama, they enjoy the drama from the bottom of their hearts. Their comment of "I want to take an IDAM session every week or every day" seems to prove the above statement.

Processes and Methods of Improvisational Drama of Acceptance and Mirroring

Two

1. OVERVIEW OF IDAM

IDAM is a well-structured approach with three parts in every session. In Part One, children play games aimed at relaxing their mind and body, and practice drama exercises so that the dramas in Part Two will be performed pleasantly and effectively. In Part Two, the therapist performs one-on-one dramas with some of the children. A drama of Jizo, the guardian deity of travelers and children, may be introduced. (Jizo is the Japanese name of one of the Bodhisattvas worshipped in Buddhism.) Part Three is designed to have the children calm down the various feelings they have felt through the dramas. Earlier, I had called Part One and Part Three the "warm-up" and "cool-down" phases, respectively. However, I now use the terms "Part One," "Part Two," and "Part Three" to prevent Part One and Part Three from being omitted to save time and to avoid the false impression that Part Two is the most important. Those parts are not supplementary. Every part is essential as an equally important process. All three parts must be conducted in each session. With each session, children evolve and deepen both individually and as a group. They enjoy the drama more abundantly and experience a feeling of liberating their inner self. The narrow definition of IDAM refers to a drama in Part Two, but the parts before and after it should always be conducted together, forming its wide definition. Please note the usage of two definitions depend on the context.

A session is structured so that children can have a good time in a reassuring atmosphere. In some cases, I conduct a session in a class of more than 40 children. While this number of children is generally regarded as too large for a drama therapy session, I have overcome this issue by designing a session where all work activities in Part One and Part Three consist only of games that everyone can play together even in a large group. I have incorporated many games in which participants imitate someone, with an awareness of mirroring, in order to create a sense of unity. Nash and Haen (2005) depict well the atmosphere that children in a drama therapy group enjoy a mirroring warm-up that

DOI: 10.4324/9781003565062-3

works as "a form of validation and attunement" (p. 125). Small children like mirroring inherently, and the games utilizing mirroring are suitable for them.

I have conducted IDAM on children between 4 and 11 years old, and it worked well. It will be applicable to younger or older children as well if the therapist forms a firm group cohesion, according to the children's state, and carefully warms up their expression activities. In fact, children as young as four years old can follow IDAM no less than older ones when they are guided through all of three parts. Only evaluation of how they interacted with activities is based on observation of the changes of their countenance and behaviors, as they are not old enough to write reflection/letters to the therapist or to have distinct self-awareness or verbalize them if any.

When school teachers lead IDAM, they need training for it, and even then, it is advisable to have a drama therapist present in sessions. To avoid multiple relationships, a teacher should choose to do IDAM in classes that they do not teach. It is necessary to exchange information on the children closely with teachers who know them well before and after each session, and to reflect on processes minutely.

The following introduces research on SBDT (school-based drama therapy), which resonates with IDAM. Frydman and Mayor (2024) conducted a scoping review "to answer the research question: What is the use and potential of SBDT to enhance socio-emotional skills in early childhood?" (p. 669) based on an extensive search and detailed evaluation.

They conclude by saying, "We recommend that school personnel receive training and consultation on SBDT and how to adopt an intentionally playful stance to support young children." I agree with their expression of a future vision "where SBDT practices and practitioners are part of the ecological fabric of schools" (p. 678), and I hope that IDAM will be included in such practices of SBDT.

Here, I will explain how to specifically proceed with IDAM.

2. BEFORE STARTING IDAM

Prior to each session, the current emotional condition of the children should be checked to see if there is anything unusual happening. For instance, when a session is conducted as an outreach activity at an elementary school or other facility, check if some event is happening there that might affect the content of the dramas. The therapist should prepare to respond to any changes in the children.

When you practice IDAM for the first time, it is important to explain to the children the purpose of IDAM and how they should participate in them. When a therapist visits an elementary school or other facility, children recognize that "it is a special time provided by an outsider," who is not their teacher or caregiver. This alone makes the session an "unusual" experience for them. However, it is necessary to clearly tell them that they can express themselves freely in the session, unlike in ordinary classes. First, you should explain to the children that there is no "correct answer" in the session. It does not matter whether they are good or bad performers or whether or not their dramas are good. Their performance is not related to their school record and they can enjoy themselves freely in the dramas. Then, you should tell children that they feel refreshed and good disregarding any such restrictions throughout the activities. (This is particularly important in a situation where all learning activities are evaluated by test scores and used to make children compete for excellence.)

When I had a review meeting with elementary school teachers who observed my session, there was a teacher who simply mentioned who had been good performers. Although I explained to the teachers the purpose of this approach in detail and had them watch many dramas, as described in this book, the relevant teacher paid attention only to whether the dramas were any good. Teachers may be used to seeing children from the perspective of whether or not they perform well, perhaps because they often evaluate them by their learning outcomes in everyday school life. However, in IDAM, I want them to pay the most attention to children's inner self and feelings. Before a session starts, therefore, it is important not only to tell children about how this will be different from their regular classes, but also to have their teachers and caregivers understand these points. I believe that if they watch children's dramas without evaluating them, they will surely find something that helps them support the children in their everyday life.

The next thing to consider is that there may be children who have no parents or who have serious problems with their parents (when IDAM is implemented in a clinical setting, there are many such cases). Since IDAM is not a drama in which children play a scene from their real family life, it does not matter whether or not they have parents. One of the ways to make children understand that drama is different from reality is to have them perform a drama under the name of "Taro" or "Hanako" (which is a common placeholder name for males or females, respectively, in Japan) instead of using their real name. Even so, if there is a child with no mother in a group, it is likely that the child would realize that they have no mother by watching a mother-child drama performed by another child. Though still only a few in Japan, there could be a gay couple family with two fathers and no mother. In such cases one solution is to allow each child to choose and designate the role that the therapist plays, such as the role of a father, mother, grandmother, grandfather, or other caregivers, without sticking to a mother-child drama.

On the other hand, children without a mother may find some insight or discovery in a mother-child drama because they may enjoy the experience of a play with a mother in their image and abstract. It is possible if a child wants and volunteers, without any pressing.

Lastly, at the beginning of each session, it is recommended to tell children that they must keep three very important promises as follows.

Promises:

1. You must cooperate with each other to play the games and must quietly watch the dramas performed by the other children.
2. You are free to do anything you like in your drama, but you must not physically attack anyone. The drama ends immediately if you use actual physical violence. (If you want to do this, you must just pretend to attack someone.)
3. Enjoy the session and feel refreshed and good!

3. PART ONE: GAMES TO ELICIT EXPRESSION AND SPONTANEITY

It is necessary to make children ready physically and mentally so that they can smoothly enter the world of drama. Activities are not just a warm-up but have many meanings and effects in themselves. Children can see an unexpected side of their classmates through their unfamiliar expressions. Moreover, the approach and receptive attitude of the therapist helps lay the foundation for them to respect each other and improve their self-esteem. A major factor that enhances the therapeutic effect is that the feelings expressed in the drama in Part Two feel authentic to the children themselves. To make this possible, Part One provides the opportunity for pre-training, for them to improve their expressive and acting abilities. However, since the activities in Part One consist of games, they appear to be far from training activities, but the children can acquire these abilities naturally through fun and laughter. Among many games, I will introduce some that I have implemented and have proven to be effective or which I have modified for the targets of IDAM. I will explain how to use the games and points to note when conducting them based on my experience. (I learned most of the games in the classes of Sally Bailey at Kansas State University. However, some of them have been devised by me. Since these games have spread to many areas from various sources, their real origins are often unknown. Although I have clarified in this book where I first learned of them, I have changed most of the names to more descriptive ones.)

① In time to music

This is a perfect game to start with as a warm-up. Children walk around a room freely to rhythmic music. They can dance, jump, or walk freely. The therapist stops the music every 10 to 20 seconds. When the music stops, the children freeze (that is, stop on the spot while maintaining their pose at that moment). When the music resumes, they begin to move again.

After they get used to doing this, they play a game called "Amoeba." They walk around and according to the number said by the therapist, divide themselves into groups with a certain number of people when the music stops. For instance, if the therapist says "three," they make a group of three people in a hurry. As soon as they can form a group, they hold hands with each other or sit down together according to the predetermined rule. The children try to form a group in a hurry so as not to fail to join a group. When the number becomes larger, such as "17," the children get really excited.

After several rounds, the therapist changes the rule and instructs them to touch together by their same body parts designated by the therapist when the music stops. For instance, if the therapist says, "elbow to elbow," they have to touch their elbow with the elbow of as many nearby classmates as possible. The therapist changes the designated body parts, including "hand to hand," "shoulder to shoulder," "ear to ear" as well as "arm to head," "shoulder to elbow," and "knee to hand." When I explained how to play this game in a class, I was asked, "If you say, 'mouth to mouth,' do we have to touch our mouths together?" When I answered that they had to do it if I said so, the class was thrown into an uproar. Every time the music stopped; everyone became momentarily alert to my instruction. Although I did not give the instruction of "mouth to mouth," this game enabled the children to relax their bodies and minds all at once in a short time while squealing in excitement. However, it should be noted that some children may have a problem with physical contact of this kind. So, the therapist should carefully conduct all activities with a good understanding and care for each child's situation.

② An imaginary yardstick

A therapist asks questions that can be answered with "yes" or "no." One end of the classroom is designated as the place for "yes," with the other end being the place for "no." Children answer the questions by moving to either place. An imaginary line is drawn on the floor in the middle of the two places and is used as a "yardstick" line. For instance, when children are asked whether they like studying or not, those who neither like nor dislike studying move to the middle point where the "yardstick" line is drawn. Similarly, children move to a place that applies to them according to how much they like or dislike studying. Questions may include: "Do you like math the most?" "Do you want to be a soccer player in the future?" "Do you like/dislike your mother?" "Are you in good physical condition today?" and "Are you sleepy now?" Unlike lessons in classes, children do not answer being seated but move around while thinking about their answer. This enables them to warm-up physically and mentally while having fun.

One significant intention on the part of the therapist is to try to obtain information on the preferences and emotional state of the children. This game can be used as a very good warm-up for the themes of the dramas that will be played in Part Two on that day. For instance, the question, "Do you have any complaints about your mother?" provides a good opportunity for children to think about it even for a short time. This enables them to express their feelings toward their mother more smoothly in a drama in Part Two.

The points to note here are that the therapist should not just ask questions only with this intention but simply ask fun questions at first to help children relax their minds and bodies, while taking into account the relationships between children in the group and the situation of their families.

③ Guess who is the leader

The therapist determines "it" (a person who is to later guess who is the leader) and asks them to go out of the classroom. Everyone forms a big circle and stands facing inward. The therapist determines the leader, taking care not to be heard by "it" outside the classroom, and asks the leader to begin to move (any action such as clapping hands, scratching their head, or stamping their feet). When everyone else begins to mirror the movement, the therapist asks "it" in. The leader changes their movement from time to time, taking care not to be noticed by "it," and everyone mirrors as quickly and unobtrusively as possible. The therapist tells the children in advance to only casually pay attention to the leader's movements, because if they are always looking at the leader, this makes it easy for "it" to know who the leader is. "It" stands in the middle of the circle, observes everyone, and guesses who the leader is. It is difficult for a child in a lower grade to play the role of "it" alone in a large class. In such a case, it is advisable that the therapist forms an "it" team with a few children and asks them to cooperate to observe the other children to guess who the leader is.

Once they get used to moving in normal motion, it is also fun to conduct the game in a dance version. The leader dances to music. Since it is difficult to imitate movements that are too complicated, the therapist asks the leader to make simple movements and not to change them too often. The game in a facial expression version is also fun. The leader makes facial expressions, and everyone mirrors them. For the game in a dance version and facial expression version, it is recommended that the therapist plays the role of the leader as an example before determining "it."

In this game, since everyone other than "it" knows who the leader is and makes the same movements as the leader while trying not to let "it" know who the leader is, they can share a sense of unity and solidarity, like accomplices in mischief. Perhaps due to this, the game is very popular with children. Many children want to play the role of the leader, in particular. This game is a good practice for fostering group-wide cooperation and serves as a very good warm-up to help them build empathy through dramas later.

However, the therapist should be careful that the child who plays "it" does not feel alienated. It is advisable that the therapist works to foster a sense of unity among the members of an "it" team, even if their number is small. Alternatively, the therapist can play the role of "it." This will be well received by children. (Origin: Game that I used to play when I was a child.)

④ Fire on the mountains

Originating in Africa, this is a game in which the leader produces a rhythm. Everyone in the class stands and forms double circles. The number of people in the outer circle and the inner circle should be the same. The leader stands in the middle of the circles and repeatedly moves their body in a steady, enjoyable rhythm. At the same time, they utter some words. They are free to utter any words or make any sounds they like. For instance, they may say "pop, pop" while flapping their arms, "tip tap" while stamping their feet, or "whew, bang" while jumping. The children forming the inner circle immediately mirror the leader's rhythm, movement, and sound together. Meanwhile, the children forming the outer circle walk or dance in one direction while keeping the circle intact. After a while, the leader stops the rhythm and movement and shouts, "Fire on the mountains!" With this signal, children in the outer circle and the inner circle pair up with a nearby person, holding hands. A pair must consist of a child in the outer circle and a child in the inner circle. After pairing up, the two can switch between the outer circle and the inner circle based on mutual consultation. Meanwhile, the leader also hurriedly looks for a partner to pair up with. If the leader can manage to find a partner, there is one person who cannot be paired with anyone. That person takes on the role of the leader the next time. In this way, the game can continue many times.

Since children may feel shy to make a rhythm or say some words all alone in the middle, those who do not want to be the leader seriously look for a partner while squealing in excitement. They seem to enjoy the thrill of that. Once, when I introduced this game after conducting several sessions, a child said to me, "Why didn't you tell us about such an interesting game sooner?" (Origin: Aycox, 1985).

⑤ Group mood guessing

This is a game in which "it" guesses what feeling or mood everyone else is expressing. The therapist determines one or two people to play "it" and asks "it" to leave the classroom. The therapist determines one feeling or mood, such as "angry" or "fun," and conveys it to everyone. In the case of an angry feeling, everyone expresses this feeling with facial expressions and body movements, for instance, by kicking the ground with their feet and clicking their tongues. The therapist immediately calls in "it" and asks them to observe everyone and guess what feeling they are expressing.

This game provides the opportunity for children to practice how to express their feelings and moods. Although it may be embarrassing for children to do this alone in front of their classmates, if it's done together with others, they can do it without being shy. If each child can express the designated feeling or mood well, "it" should be able to guess the correct answer immediately. However, even if children are instructed to express anger, some children do not appear to be angry at all. Accordingly, it is strongly recommended that when playing this game for the first time, the therapist first expresses various feelings and have the children guess what feelings are being expressed. It is advisable to make children practice how to express feelings a little exaggeratedly.

It is also important to tell children that they should express the designated feeling in an easy-to-understand way so that "it" can guess the correct answer. Otherwise, some children intentionally show a confusing expression to prevent "it" from guessing the correct answer immediately. In such a case, "it" is confused and cannot reach the correct answer. Another point to note is they should be prohibited from using words. It does not serve well the purpose of this game, even if "it" can guess the correct answer, by hearing someone say, "He's driving me crazy."

When the children get used to playing this game, it is recommended to make them try to express feelings that are harder to guess, such as "embarrassed" or "hungry." When "it" becomes able to guess the correct answer smoothly, both "it" and everyone else begins to concentrate on the game and enjoy it more. This is a great practice opportunity for them to learn how to express their feelings with the body and facial expressions and understand the feelings of others (Origin: Emunah, 2020, p. 166–167).

⑥ Gesture telephone game

In a normal telephone game, participants are divided into several teams and whisper the same message from one person to the next until it gets to the last person. Each team competes for how well the message is communicated to the last person. I have come up with the gesture version, thinking that it may be interesting to play it using gestures, not words. Since the children communicate a message only with body movements, those who are not good at verbally communicating their feelings and what they want to say like this game.

Several teams of five or six people are lined up in a row. The therapist asks those first in line to come near them and shows a certain act only with gestures and facial expressions. At this time, the others wait, turning to face the other side of the classroom, so that they cannot see the gestures of the therapist. After understanding the message communicated by the therapist, the people first in line return to their respective teams. They ask only the second person to look back and communicate the message with gestures. The therapist has to make them follow the rule of not saying anything at this time so that they do not explain the message verbally. Then, the third person looks back to receive the message from the second person and communicates it to the next person. In this way, the message is communicated in turn until it gets to the last person. Finally, the last person of each team shows the message with gestures in front of all members. Then, the therapist shows the original gestures that they had shown to the people first in line in front of everyone, and the team that most closely acted the original gestures wins the game.

It is important to tell the children not to ask the previous person what gesture they made, even if they cannot remember it, and not to tell the next person that they are making a different gesture.

The therapist sees to it that the gestures are based on a familiar, short stories. Some examples are: "In a baseball game, a batter swings and misses once, hits a home run the second time, and crosses the home plate with a big smile," "A person drops one of their contact lenses, searches hard for it with one eye, and finally finds it," "In a priority seat on a train, a person gives up their seat to an elderly person."

Most children love this game, even though they may want to avoid standing out and making a gesture, especially the last child in the line, who has to show the gesture in front of everyone. However, as they get used to playing the game, they enjoy it very much. A child wrote the following impression:

> Since I was shy, I didn't want to be the last person. I was a little hesitant to make a gesture, but at the same time I enjoyed it. As I made the gesture while wondering why I felt that way, I overcame my shyness. Since then, I haven't hesitated to take on the role of the last person.

Above all, it is important for the therapist to make a bold gesture without being shy when first showing it. (Origin: The game was devised by me.)

⑦ One hundred faces with "Oh"

In this game, children emotionally express their feelings with gestures, using only the interjection "Oh," which can be said and expressed in different ways according to various feelings and situations. (I used "Ah" instead of "Oh" because it is common in Japan.)

Everyone forms a big circle. Anyone who comes up with an idea takes a step forward and says "Oh" with gestures without explaining anything. Although they may say "Oh" in any way depending on the situation, including pronouncing it short or long like "Ohhhh" and repeating it several times, they are allowed to say only one word: "Oh." They must not say any other words. Other children mirror the way the performer said, "Oh" with gestures all together, imagining what kind of situation the performer was in, and share how they felt at that time. The performer does not have to explain what kind of situation they were in, and the other children do not have to ask. By expressing their feelings, saying "Oh" in various ways, even for a moment, the children can realize that there are various ways of saying even a single word. They can also experience and enjoy empathy and a sense of unity by mirroring the performance together. Regarding the performer, even shy children seem to feel reassured because everyone imitates them immediately after they perform.

There are various scenes in everyday life in which a person says, "Oh," such as: "Oh!" when finding something good while walking down the road. "Oh!" when suddenly remembering something (however, there is a big difference between remembering that they forgot their pencils while going to school and remembering that they forgot to turn off the stove while on the go). "Oh" when being disappointed in their expectations, and "Ohh" when finding that their younger brother has eaten their snacks.

When the game is conducted for the first time, it is recommended that the therapist shows an example because this is the easiest way for the children to understand. However, the therapist should not show many examples because it is important that the children come up with their own ideas. In some cases, children put on an amazing performance using "Oh." In this sense as well, this is a game that lets us have fun. (Origin: Theatre workshop led by Tomio Narisawa and Setsu Hanasaki.)

⑧ A scene from daily life

In this game, children play a very short scene from their daily life with gestures and words. The method of this game is almost the same as for "One hundred faces with Oh." Everyone forms a big circle. Anyone who comes up with an idea takes a step forward inside the circle and plays a short scene from their daily life with dialogue for a few to ten seconds.

Immediately after the performance, everyone mirrors it. However, to prevent them from mirroring it too playfully in a chaotic atmosphere, the therapist should ask the performer what scene they played and instruct everyone to share their feeling at that time. Some children pick up a scene which gives them very significant emotions like some of the scenes below.

The following are a few examples of scenes that children have played:

- When I got home, I unlocked the door myself and said, "I'm home." There was no reply because there was no one at home.
- I yelled at my younger brother, "Stop playing with my toys!"
- I went for a walk with my dog, saying, "John, come on!"
- When I was told by my mother to go shopping, I turned around and bumped into a chest.

Everyone plays these scenes all together, saying the same words, just as the performer did. Although the class becomes noisy, they enjoy doing it. However, children sometimes play too much. If one child plays a scene in which they slip and fall, the other children will begin to play a similar scene. This is good in a sense because they have fun. However, if everyone falls, this may pose a risk to the children. Therefore, the therapist should be careful not to let them go in such directions with risky behavior or with practical jokes.

Many children list this game as an impressive and fun game in their reflective letters written to me later. They are pleased to have everyone else play the same scene all together just as they did. This game brings empathy and a sense of unity to children. In addition, by getting used to acting through this game, children can enter the world of improvisational drama more smoothly in Part Two. (Origin: The game was devised by me as a developed version of "One hundred faces with Oh.")

⑨ All-participation-type word association game

This is a game in which everyone says a word that comes to mind all together. In a normal word association game, one answerer says a word that they associate with the word that the questioner gives as a hint. In this game, everyone says a word that has come to mind all at once. In addition, since there is no correct answer, each child can give their own answer. As another feature, there is a rule that allows children to use not only a noun or other word but also any other way of expressing what they think. Accordingly, the children shout aloud what they want to say freely with delight. For instance, when I say the word "school," the children shout things like "Friends!" "Fun!" "I don't want to go!" When I say the word "mother," they shout, "I love Mom!" "I want her to buy me a game!" "Scary!" and "Noisy hag!" Since everyone speaks all at once, they do not make out or even listen to what each other is saying, which will give them utmost relief. Whenever I explain to children how to play this game, I just tell them to *say* what has come to their mind. However, every child, without exception, *shouts* as loudly as possible. It even seems that they relieve stress by saying what they want to say in their own world. Above all, they look very refreshed, which, in turn, makes me feel happy.

If I know that there is a child who has some problem, I say a word related to the child so that they can express their thoughts verbally. In such a case, I sometimes clearly feel that they spit out negative energy. By listening to what they say, I can also understand how they feel about it. It was in this game that **A**, who was mentioned in the Introduction, happily shouted "Poop!"

This game can be used not only as a warm-up but also as a cooldown. It is also useful when the therapist wants the children to let out something left unsaid or undone during their dramas or clear away any frustration that they felt when watching their classmates' dramas, or to just release excess energy. When this game is conducted at the end of a session, it is advisable to have the children determine what they will say (such as "I'm hungry!" and "It was fun!") and say it all at once. This enables them to settle their minds, make them realize that the session is over, and also to gain a feeling of satisfaction. (Origin: The game was devised by me.)

⑩ Let's count up to 21!

In this game, the children as a group have to count from one to 21. Each child says one number at a time in turn. However, they have to try it without any discussion about who says "one" or "two," etc. The goal of the game is to count up to 21 without overlapping. Specifically, X says "one," Y says "two," and then Z says "three." However, if Y and Z say "three" at the same time, the children have to count from "one" again. This game requires concentration and cooperation. This is a profound game through which participants can learn about various human relationships and communication skills, including how to read the room and others' intentions, and how to actively express themselves in a spirit of mutual concession. Even if it is played by adults, it follows a very interesting process. If there is even one person who does not carefully look for the right time to say the next number, it is not easy to reach 21. On the other hand, if they are all too reserved, the game does not go smoothly, either.

If this game is played by children, in particular, in a large class, it is difficult to even count to five. Compared to adults, more children are willing to say the numbers. Meanwhile, some children are slow to realize that they should stay quiet for a while because the game does not go forward if they keep saying numbers. There are also some children who do not stop saying the numbers even if they do realize it. It often happens that several children always say the number at the same time, and, as a result, the children cannot even count to two.

However, if the therapist encourages them to stop talking and concentrate on the game, the game has an amazing effect. As they get used to playing the game and are able to count to larger numbers, they are single-minded and concentrate only on counting the numbers, forgetting everything else. In that sense, this game is rather more suitable as a way to resolve children's feelings than being used as warm-up.

I feel that by concentrating only on counting the numbers in the game, children are led to being here and now, and forget unagreeable effects, if any, that might have occurred in their mind and wash away their feelings, making them feel refreshed. Since number 21 is almost too difficult to reach, the therapist may begin by setting a lower goal for the moment, such as "up to five" or "up to 10." Then, children can gain a sense of accomplishment when they are able to achieve the goal through cooperation with each other. They can also share a sense of unity as a group and finish the session in a very good mood (Origin: Aycox, 1985).

Key points for Part One

Select a few of the above games for a session. (Other games are also available. It is better if a game can bring about a greater sense of unity and has an element of mirroring.) Make a plan so that the first game to play in each session is the same, some number of same games are conducted every time, games are arranged in a developmental sequence, and the skills acquired through these games are effective for drama acting in the sessions.

In 5. Group mood guessing, I recommend that the therapist first expresses various feelings in front of children. Not only for this game, but for any game, it is very important that the drama therapist shows an example, especially in the first session for the children. You should show your performance first, and not let the children act without first seeing yours.

I always feel that children's eyes light up when they see a therapist give a performance. This not only inspires their performance but also helps them feel familiar with and respect the therapist. This enabled me to proceed with Part Two very smoothly. It is also very effective to perform a story in the first session. This helps children enter the world of imagination at once and proceed with the process of their performing a drama smoothly.

4. PART TWO: IMPROVISATIONAL DRAMA OF ACCEPTANCE AND MIRRORING

Now our topic moves to a one-on-one drama with a child. I will first explain the difference between IDAM and Developmental Transformations because some may think that they are similar. When I developed IDAM, I had not yet learned about Developmental Transformations. I later received training on it from David Johnson and other teachers. The first major difference is that in IDAM, games and work activities other than improvisational dramas are structured and that a therapist and a child perform a very short drama for a few minutes only once, in principle, playing the fixed role of a mother and a child, respectively. The second difference is that each short drama is played in front of all the children of the group and watched (witnessed) by them. Meanwhile, the following are the important common principles of these two approaches. A drama therapist, "not as a sidecoach or director, but as an actor from within the play" (Johnson, 2009, p. 95) encounters a child in a setting where there are no stage props or toys. What is important here is that the therapist encourages the client to continue their journey "by showing spontaneity, creativity, and humor through their healing charisma" (Johnson, 2009, p. 95). Regarding the methods, repetition (mirroring) is common among the several methods used in Developmental Transformations and is used for the same purpose as in IDAM. Here, "repetition (mirroring)" refers to "immediate repetition or mirroring of dramatic elements observed in the client's behavior, including movement qualities, sounds, or images. The leader picks up on what is present" (Johnson, 2005, p. 17). In IDAM, it is the most important and fundamental element to accept the content of children's story and to mirror both their positive and negative feelings in a short drama. For children, IDAM exists as a time and space to confront the problem they are facing enjoyably. Though its aim is not to resolve their problem, it makes children feel better by providing them with a therapeutic moment in many cases.

1. Drama setting

I reaffirm that it is significant that they can have the experience of sharing a good mood with a therapist in a drama in which the therapist deals with their true feelings even though it is a fictional setting. The following process is packed into a short time frame: a therapist first creates a situation of conflict or confrontation, where they make children fully express their feelings, and then helps them resolve their feelings. If the process is successfully completed, IDAM deserves to be called, literally, super brief drama therapy.

First, you determine a simple scene as follows: a mother tells her child to go to school at once, or a mother, bringing some snacks to her child's room after school, tells them to do their homework or study harder. These two scenes encourage Japanese children to express their feelings of rebellion and conflict against their mother. Any other scenes that are likely to occur in daily life are good. You should avoid a complicated setting.

Next, you determine only the first action and words (for instance, a mother looks at the clock and says to her child, "You'll be late. Go to school at once.").

You then tell children to come forward if they want to volunteer to perform a drama. You should not designate someone because the children's spontaneity should be valued. In the end, it sometimes happens that "regulars" perform the dramas more often than not. Even in such a case, if you create an atmosphere in which all children share the same experience in Part One, children who are not proactive and always just watch others perform can also feel a sense of unity because they *proactively* watch them as part of the audience and *emotionally participate*. This sense of unity creates the same effect in those just watching others play. Shteynberg (2015) states that synchronous, shared attention with others produces memories, emotions, and motivations at a more profound level. Therefore, even if children do not actually perform a drama, they can receive some benefit. Mirroring does not occur only between the therapist and the child who perform the drama together, but also with the audience. Above could be some explanation that children are moved in their heart and get healing, and they can feel, think, and learn something by witnessing others' stories in dramas. Since Japan is a collective-minded country, watching someone's drama together is better suited, and it is one of the strengths of IDAM. Shteynberg and Apfelbaum (2013) say that shared attention enables people to learn from the behavior of others and get more imitation. In addition to stimulation, by watching a drama performed by others, children are likely to volunteer to play later. These changes of attitude often lead many of them to become more active in their regular classes and in their daily lives. For the performing child, in turn, the mirroring of the affect by the therapist and audience validates the child and provides a witnessing of their lived experience. Witnessing is one of drama therapy's core healing elements.

When starting a drama, you should always follow the same routine, including slapping your hands together once, saying, "Let's start," in order to have the children clearly recognize the beginning of the drama. Then, you perform a one-on-one drama with a child in full view of classmates as the audience. Once a situation is set up, it should be applied in the same way as many times as there comes forward a child who wants to play it. As you continue, the same solid framework is to be maintained with your starting the scene with the same action and words whoever you play with. The key point is to never leave the scene setting to the children and, conversely, always allow them to perform the drama freely after it commences. For the subsequent flow, please refer to the many drama examples as described in the following chapters. Each drama should be from about one to a few minutes long. If you respond to the behavior of the children, a drama automatically follows the four-part organization of Japanese narratives of introduction, development, turn, and ending (see Chapter Four for details). Thus, there often comes a time when you feel that one drama episode has reached an ending. It is at this time that you should bring the drama to an end. Use the same routine such as saying, "This is the end of the drama," and everyone claps their hands together to show appreciation to the performing child. The reason for using the same routine at the beginning and the end of a drama is to make a clear distinction between reality and drama by using ceremonial power. If the children understand when they are entering or exiting their own role, they will recognize when the therapist plays the role of a mother and then returns to being a therapist. It is also recommended to have the children perform dramas under the same names, such as "Taro" and "Hanako," and to call them by their correct given name after the drama ends so that they can distinguish between their actual self and their role.

2. Proceeding with the drama story

You should listen to what children express in a drama with all your heart and soul, understanding what feelings are directed at you. It is most important to accept the words, actions, and feelings of children without any criticism or judgment. Although this is the same attitude as that of counseling techniques based on acceptance and empathic understanding in client-centered therapy developed by Rogers (1951), IDAM is embodied in the form of a drama. This, however, is easy to say and difficult to do since you manage a drama while at once playing opposite a child and proceeding with the story.

In real practices, there are cases where you cannot or do not have to both accept and mirror the child's behavior at the same time. It is often appropriate to do either one or the other. For instance, when I (see the case story of **I** in Chapter Four) said in a drama that he was sore all over, I showed my acceptance not by mirroring his pain, but rather by giving him a massage. Meanwhile, in most cases where I cannot immediately accept the behavior or feelings of children who direct their anger at me (the mother), I mirror their behavior or feelings (or words in some cases). For instance, when children express rebellious feelings, stamping their feet, saying that they do not want to study, the mother in the drama stamps her feet, while creating the *same kind* of mood as theirs, and tells them to study harder. It is not necessary to tell them that they do not have to study. If you say that, they may be unable to fully express their rebellious energy during the drama. It is important and difficult to determine how to respond to them in such a scene. If you feel that the children do not want to study or want to rebel against the mother, it is important that you create the *same kind* of feeling and mood to make them release such energy. Moreover, in order to make them even more rebellious, you might tell them to study harder as the mother. Although you may have a conflict with the children about studying, you should match your feelings and behavior to those of the children. If you feel that the children's rebellious feeling against the mother is not so intense, you can express a desire familiar to children, such as a wish not to cook dinner, so as to share the same negative feeling with them. This can bring an interesting turn to the drama. Although the responses in the above two cases are different, the basic idea is that you should reflect the *same kind* of feelings and behavior as the children and then return such feelings and behavior back to them, thereby accepting them. If the children are depressed, you should also express a depressed mood. If the children are excited in delight, you should respond with a similar mood. As shown in Chapter One, the important point is that the therapist should keep their emotional level a little lower than children's. That is why I used the term "*same kind*" in the above description.

You should be careful, in particular, when dealing with anger. It is dangerous if your act of acceptance and mirroring only results in raising the angry tension of the children. Therefore, you should keep your emotional level a little lower, as described above, and only "pretend" to be angry. You also have to find out how much energy the children have and whether it would be refreshing for the children or escalate them more if they let it out at that point. Even if children talk tough, they may actually be feeling depressed. If you react to their words and mirror them with a strong attitude, they may be frightened. At such times, you should mirror their mood because their body and facial expressions express their feelings more faithfully than their words. You must never inflate their feelings. All of these judgements sometimes require very delicate sense on the therapist's part. Therefore, if you are not sure how to evaluate such cases, it is recommended that you refine your sensitivity through additional training before conducting this approach. It is necessary for a drama therapist to have this kind of sensitivity. You should focus your attention on the overall mood and feelings emanating from the child's body (the firmness and softness of their posture, etc.). Your clear intention and mental attitude to mirror children based on what you feel from them enables the drama to have a satisfying development for them.

Next, it is imperative that you treat every child equally. This means that you should treat all dramas with equal care, interact with equal sincerity and communicate with equal energy. This is again easier said than done. One may tend to place more weight on or praise dramas that are interesting or appealing from the perspective of the audience and a general point of view as well as dramas that children perform well. However, this must be avoided by all means.

When you feel that it is difficult to develop a drama in some meaningful way during your early stage of practice, you do not need to change the direction of the drama or hurriedly bring some conclusion to the drama. Please always recognize that it is significant in itself to simply mirror/repeat the same thing over and over. If you continue to accept the child, this often helps bring about changes in their mind little by little and eventually let them feel amicable.

3. Ensuring that a therapist plays opposite a child

In creative arts therapies other than drama therapy, a play therapist plays with a client, a dance therapist dances with a client, and a music therapist sings and plays a musical instrument with a client. In this discipline, therapists share some activities with clients to activate them and stimulate their responses, thereby helping them transform themselves. Although a drama therapist sometimes just serves as a facilitator or director without sharing activities with a client, basically it is essential and natural for a drama therapist to perform a drama with them.

A therapist playing opposite a child is crucial as the therapist can directly feel and understand the child's feelings by performing a drama together, as discussed in Chapter Four. It is very important that the therapist be able to get in touch with children's true feelings by playing opposite them. Only when a therapist plays opposite a child can they understand whether or not the child is just acting to elicit laughs from their classmates. Furthermore, a therapist's playing opposite children enables them to protect the client. Basically, it is recommended that a drama should not be performed only by children. If a therapist lets children proceed with the story of a drama themselves, they might hurt their opposite because some children may become aggressive or suddenly use violence. When a drama turns that way, the children are no longer performers in a drama but become real perpetrators or victims. When I actually let children perform a drama on their own in the early days of my practice, I ended up having to really mediate quarrels. Even with adults, when the population has difficulty distinguishing between drama and reality, they may also turn out to need my arbitration of quarrels. By contrast, there are few such concerns in dramas with a script. For instance, there is a big difference between how children's feelings are hurt when they play the role of a child who is bullied in a drama with a script, and when they do so in an improvisational drama. The difference lies in that their feelings are less likely to be hurt when a performer attacks them with words memorized from a script.

Key points for Part Two

Thus, in Part Two of IDAM, the therapist plays opposite a child so that the child can fully do whatever they want to do. At the same time, develop the drama toward eventual closure. If no closure comes, you will end the drama after letting them fully repeat the same behavioral pattern.

5. PART THREE: CLOSURE PROCESS

In the case of sessions for children, unlike sessions for adults, it is very easy to get them warmed up physically and mentally. Children are always ready to play. Conversely, the process of closing a session is much more important and sometimes difficult.

1. Deroling and de-emotion

The process of safely closing a session includes the procedure of "deroling," through which players return to their real self from the role that they played in the drama. However, I want to be careful using this term. It is relatively easy for any performer (if there is no pathological factor) to derole themselves, by distinguishing between drama and reality, and confirming that they have returned to their real self. However, even after returning to their real self, they are still under the influence of the character in the drama and have the feelings of the character left inside. If these are negative feelings, it is important to "wash them away." I have named this concept and its procedure "de-emotion." The procedures for deroling do not automatically effectuate de-emotion at once. Even if the performers can derole themselves from a role, the emotions generated in a drama may still remain with a child in many cases. If there are children who appear to be still in an aggressive mood or have strong anger, the therapist must take responsibility for consciously settling down such feelings and guide them to bring back positive feelings into real life. The audience members should also need the procedure of deroling and de-emotion because "[t]he witnesses are imaginatively and emotionally transported into the scene and vicariously take on the roles and emotions" (Dickinson & Bailey, 2024, p. 140). That is why Part Three is essential.

Another point that is often overlooked is that it is necessary not only to derole players themselves but also to derole them from the perspective of their classmates. I call this "deroling from others' eyes." Some children may fall into believing that a child who played an undesirable role is really such a strange person only because of his playing that role in the drama. The therapist must restore the child's original image for the group.

Elements that are thought to be useful for children's growth and improvement of their quality of life (QoL), such as a good mood and self-confidence, are to be brought back to real life without being washed away. However, even if children are in a good mood, it is important to conduct Part Three to prevent them from remaining too excited.

2. Activities for closure

Quoting Jones (2007), Lassken (2017) describes the nature of closure as "separate from de-roling and yet both belong to the completion phase of a drama therapy session." This means that ritualistic activities contribute to a safe closure of sessions and facilitation of deroling.

The recommended activities for the closure process are those in which children can gain a sense of unity through solidarity and concentration. They include the "Let's count up to 21!" game, and using music that children like. When you choose dancing or singing to music for the purpose of closing a session, it is advisable to use the same dance with the same movement or the same song. Other example rituals for deroling include shaking off or brushing off a role, calling the actors' own names out loud, and saying goodbye to the space (Lassken, 2017). This is the similar process that professional actors unconsciously follow. They return to their real self from the character in a drama through their routine of taking off a costume or makeup after finishing their act onstage. Even if there are children who are deeply involved in the drama of the day, it is possible to quickly settle down their feelings by creating in them such a sense that "Oh, this music is ringing, so our drama time is over," like a conditioned response. The therapist also plays in a drama in IDAM, and should not forget to derole themself as well, when deemed necessary. One good way of deroling I recommend for the therapist is to enjoy Part Three together with children.

It is ideal to take time for children to express their impressions in addition to conducting games, etc. The purpose of this process is to allow children to express any residual sensation and settle down should they be still under the effect of negative feelings from the role they played. It is also effective for them to confirm that they have returned to their real self from the character in the drama by expressing their impressions and to have their classmates confirm it. If it is found from their impressions that children have gained a positive perspective and self-confidence, it is important for the therapist to provide supportive comments that strengthen them.

In my case, in order to prevent children from going home immediately after a session without completely settling their feelings, I make it a rule to conduct a session before lunch time and eat school lunch together with the children. Even if there are children who cannot calm down their excitement, lunch time provides the opportunity for them to cool down and prepares them to participate in an afternoon class without any trouble.

It is also highly recommended to have children write down their impressions or in a form of a letter to the therapist at a later date. These impressions can have them notice changes in themselves in their own way to verbalize and evaluate what has happened to them. In their impressions, many children expressed regret over the fact that they could not receive drama therapy sessions anymore because I am from outside the school. There seems to be a possibility that they can categorize my sessions as an "enjoyable memory" by writing a letter to me and may take advantage of that memory in some form in the future.

Key points for Part Three

The closure process is essential. Although some effort is made to have the children distinguish between drama and reality in Part Two, you should conduct a closure work in Part Three. Your task is to set a clear boundary upon and contain children's negative feelings coming from the influence of a drama or feelings that should not connect to reality, while you enhance the children's positive feelings and behavior patterns. It is effective to combine several activities (games, rituals, time to express impressions, etc.). It is essential that you end the whole process with the intention of firmly "closing" the session.

6. THE IMPORTANCE OF STRUCTURE AND FORMS IN IDAM

At first glance, IDAM may appear to be an approach conducted widely and shallowly because it deals with the members of an entire group all at once in as few as three sessions. Indeed, the effective functioning of the *structure and form* of IDAM can bring about a deep and meaningful process for many children. From the results of my practice so far, it is thought that the initial purpose of making children express negative feelings, release stress, and gain good feelings has been achieved. In addition,

I have frequently seen its significant healing effects even if only a few sessions are conducted. Above all, it is excellent that children are very pleased to participate in IDAM sessions. The therapist deals with various problems facing children just through acceptance and mirroring in a short, condensed period of time. In a sense, the "space" offered by IDAM has the function of reflecting the existence of each child as a whole. This very "space" is the life of IDAM.

To recapitulate, the structure of IDAM is as follows.

Part One: The therapist conducts playful mutual interaction and warms up body, mind, and relations of all children in a class (or group members).

Part Two: As all the children come to feel better and much closer to each other, the therapist then is able to create a situation with a safe framework by allocating such peer group members as witnesses or supporters. The audience watches as witnesses of the emotional resonance and interaction between two performers, which are produced through mirroring in a drama. This structure functions for these children in a similar way as those who attend or watch a wedding ceremony or watch a sports team's perfectly coordinated performance. Under these circumstances, each child performs an improvisational drama of mother and child, in which they express their feelings through conflict (in many cases), has them accepted, and overcomes them. Following this drama, a Jizo drama is conducted, in which children express their dreams and hopes. The effects of these dramas also spread to children who participate in them only as the audience.

Part Three: The sense of unity among the children has been increased. The therapist closes the process while maintaining their sense of unity.

The next important factor is the form of IDAM. Since drama therapy is basically group therapy (although one-on-one sessions with a therapist are also conducted), it has the advantage of promoting participants to grow together by making good use of group dynamics. Featuring a unique form, IDAM is neither an individual session nor a session in which all participants participate in all activities. Since an improvisational drama is performed by one child at a time, each drama seems to be independent from each other in form. However, the same content and feelings (for instance, rebellious feelings against the mother or words such as, "I don't want to go to school") are repeatedly expressed by different children one after another. This repetition is not just imitation but is actually a necessary process for the entire IDAM process. Each drama inevitably changes after its initial opening and becomes unique to each child. When a series of dramas are viewed as a whole, it is found that they develop while creating a single process. To explain this process in relation to the action of mirror neurons, it clearly follows that IDAM has a structure that will easily facilitate the development of drama, and mutual growth and healing of participants through its setting where mirror neurons of audience children are greatly activated and reflected both ways between the audience and the drama as they watch the therapist and one child perform it. In this sense, in IDAM, children watching dramas can be called co-creators, not just the audience.

7. PRACTICAL STEPS AND SUMMARY OF INSTRUCTIONS

The following is a simple summary of practical steps and instructions. The flow of one typical session is shown below. It is recommended that a session be conducted at least three times (once a week is optimal) and that it be 60 or 90 minutes long, depending on the situations of the facilities.

① Check the condition of the children (mental and physical condition, recent events, etc.).
② Explain to the children the purpose of performing this drama ("I want you to enjoy a drama, to relieve stress in a drama").
③ Clearly tell the children in the first session how many sessions will be conducted in total.
④ Never skip any process and always conduct all parts from Part One through Part Three in each session.
⑤ Present and confirm three promises.

Part One: Conduct some of the following games or similar games:

1. In time to music
2. An imaginary yardstick
3. Guess who is the leader
4. Fire on the mountains
5. Group mood guessing
6. Gesture telephone game
7. One hundred faces with "Oh"
8. A scene from daily life
9. All-participation-type word association game
10. Let's count up to 21!

The therapist must incorporate such a process of first showing a performance themself for children to see and enjoy. They demonstrates a model before conducting a game that requires the expression of feelings, and performs a story before children start performing.

Part Two

1. Set up a scene of an improvisational drama.

   The therapist plays the role of a mother/primary caregiver, and the child plays the role of her daughter or son.

   Determine a specific scene and the first action and words (which should be simple).

   Set up a scene that is easy to provoke conflict, if possible.

   Never leave the scene setting to the children.

   Make sure that the role of the child and the relationships between the roles in a drama are different from their real-life situation.

   Do not deal with actual issues occurring on the spot or within the relevant group.

2. Perform a drama with the children, one child at a time, for one to several minutes, in front of everyone.

   Perform a drama with a child who volunteers (do not designate a performer).

   Start the drama by doing the same thing every time, such as slapping your hands together once.

   Allow the child to perform the drama completely freely once the drama starts.

   Ensure that a therapist plays opposite the child (a drama should not be performed only by children).

   Accept/mirror the child's behavior, feelings, and mood.

   For acceptance and mirroring, the therapist has to keep their emotional level lower than the child's, and face the child with an intention to contain the child's expressions.

   Accept anything that a child expresses in a drama, no matter what it is.

   Even if the same thing appears (in the same drama or even if it is repeated in another drama by another child), the therapist accepts the repetition.

   See to it that the therapist is not too committed to acting.

   Keep in mind to lead the drama to be child centered.

   Do not give the drama an ending that the therapist comes up with.

Never force the child to let out their feelings.

Do not rate the child's performance in a drama.

Make sure to treat every drama equally.

Pay attention to the feelings expressed by the child, not to whether the child performs the drama well.

When mirroring, place priority on the child's body movements, facial expressions, and mood if there is a difference between their words and feelings.

End every drama with fixed words and actions, such as "The end!" and slapping your hands once loudly, etc.

Everyone claps their hands at the end of each drama to show appreciation.

3. After all children who volunteer perform a drama, the therapist changes the drama setting.
4. A Jizo drama should be conducted in at least one session or more. (Better to be put in the last session if only one Jizo drama is conducted.)

Part Three: Conduct activities for closing the session.

1. Rituals for deroling, and other activities such as "Let's count up to 21!" game, dancing, and singing.
2. Each child shares their impressions with other children in a group. Have them write their impressions at a later date.
3. Watch over the state of the children after they perform a drama.
4. The therapist reviews and considers each drama.

How Do Children Heal Themselves through IDAM?

Three

IDAM is conducted mainly with the following four purposes:

(1) Expressing feelings and achieving catharsis
(2) Fostering imagination, creativity, and improving self-esteem
(3) Realizing what participants cannot do in real life
(4) Experiencing empathy with peers and a pleasant sense of unity

By working to achieve these four purposes, you will be able to increase children's self-esteem, improvisation skills, spontaneity, expressiveness, and interpersonal relationships. This leads to improving holistic ability to live.

I will now show how to achieve the above purposes, giving examples.

1. EXPRESSING FEELINGS AND ACHIEVING CATHARSIS

Children almost always reflect their feelings in a drama even if they are not conscious of what their feelings are. By accepting their feelings, a therapist aims to encourage children to express them and achieve catharsis.

In a fourth-grade class, I set up a scene of a home in the morning. I performed with 12 different children. Every time, I started by telling a child to go to school at once so as not to be late. Every child rebelled against going to school, giving reasons such as, "My school bag is broken" and "I lost my textbook." In most cases, a child's emotional expression and the settlement of a drama were realized in a few minutes. **B** is one of the active participants in the sessions and he always behaved aggressively. Below is one such drama with him.

"Shut up! You fool!"

Mother:	Hurry up, hurry up. You'll be late for school.
B:	Shut up! Be quiet! (*Although he was seated on a chair, he was so agitated that as soon as the drama started, he kicked the chair with one foot while staring hard at me.*)

DOI: 10.4324/9781003565062-4

Mother:	Why are you doing that? *(Expressing the same angry emotion but at the lower level than his, I mirrored his action and kicked a chair with one foot as he had done.)*
	The audience enjoyed the drama as always, laughing happily and interrupting with cheers, as if they were watching a comedy.
B:	*(He kept staring at me with fixed eyes.)*
	His mood did not seem to change and his energy remained strong. I decided to change the atmosphere and my emotion to see how he reacted.
Mother:	*(With my hands on my chest, I made a sad face and talked in a small voice.)* I'm shocked.
B:	*(In a mood of refusing my attitude)* That doesn't work for me! *(He kept staring at me.)*
Mother:	You hate me, don't you?
	(He stared at me with such serious and scary eyes. I felt his strong feeling of anger. Later, when I objectively watched the video taken at the time, it seemed that we were pleasantly performing a drama with the audience still laughing, and that I had emotional leeway. In fact, however, at the time we did the scene, I didn't feel as if I had that luxury.)
B:	Shut up! You fool! *(He lifted the chair slightly as if he were trying to brandish it.)*
Audience:	*(shouting)* He's scary! He's a bad boy!
B:	I don't have to go to school! *(He put one foot on the seat of the chair and threatened me.)*
Mother:	*(Smiling a little to ease his tension, but mirroring his behavior and way of talking)* How come? You have to go to school and study.
B:	*(He immediately hit me in the face. In fact, he just pretended to do so. He knew full well that he was performing a drama.)*
Mother:	*(I crouched and cried, covering my face with my hands, while avoiding creating a serious mood.)* I never intended to raise you like this. *(A little pause. Talking to myself)* Did I really raise him like this?
B:	Yeah.
Mother:	*(Hearing him immediately answer in that way, I honestly felt as the mother in the drama that it was my fault that he had accumulated so much anger.)* Well, I'm sure there was something wrong with me.

One of the audience members:	Now you know! *(He might have been mirroring **B**'s feelings or thinking of his own mother.)*
Mother:	*(With a little smile, I addressed the relevant boy.)* I didn't ask for your opinion. *(By doing this, I intended to ease **B**'s tension. While continuing to crouch, I intertwined my fingers on my chest as if I were praying. I said to **B** with a gentle tone, looking up at him.)* I'll become a better mother as much as possible from now on and will not tell you to hurry up. I want you to be a better boy, too.
B:	*(He suddenly got into a gentle and childlike mood.)* It would have been nice if you had said so from the beginning.
Mother:	*(I showed that I was happy and smiled. I stood up and talked to him gently.)* I know you are doing your best. I won't tell you to hurry up, but I want you to go to school.
B:	*(After thinking for a moment, he said quietly)* I burned a textbook.
Mother:	*(I felt that he wanted to continue to perform the drama while interacting with his mother and spoke to him gently.)* Well then, I'm going to clear my mind and buy another textbook for you. So let's make up, shall we? *(I looked into his face.)*
B:	*(After a moment, he nodded quietly but clearly.)*
Mother:	*(Feeling very happy.)* Oh, you're a good boy, **B**. *(I spontaneously held his head with my hands. The drama ended there.)*

In a short time (two and a half minutes), I did my utmost to face his entire personality and felt a sense of accomplishment, as if I had resolved a long-standing conflict with him. This was my honest feeling at that time.

At the beginning of the drama, I did not suggest reconciliation as the mother because I wanted to make him express his anger. In the drama, I spontaneously said to him, "You hate me, don't you?" This intense expression further stimulated his feelings and immediately led to his offensive behavior. This enabled us to firmly confront each other. If we had not done so, he would have felt that he did not fully express his feelings and would have remained frustrated. In such a case, we may not have gained the genuine pleasure felt through reconciliation in the end. However, the readers should note that I tried to calm him a little in the drama so that his feelings would not become too strong (by relaxing my face and returning to my real self to talk to the audience while mirroring his angry actions and words).

When I told the homeroom teacher that I was concerned about **B**'s aggressive utterance always appearing in a drama, he replied, "He is a good boy, without any problems at school and at home." A homeroom teacher is well informed of situations on children, the amount of which is incomparable to mine, as I spend only a short time with them. It will be true if the teacher says he is a good boy. Yet, the emotions coming out of the child were true too in a drama as short as just one minute. And, if **B** becomes aggressive every time, it means that he has some negative energy within. IDAM is capable of discovering and allowing expression of latent emotions at an early stage in children who may not be apparent to hold negative energy in relation to day-to-day life.

The case of **B** is just one example. In my experience, the aggression and violence of children have often settled in the process of letting them express themselves and accepting them in a drama.

"Let's tear up the textbooks!"

The following is the case of **C**.

Of the 12 children who wanted to perform the drama, **C** volunteered later than the others. Although she had enjoyed games that everyone played together, she had strongly refused to play a game she had to perform alone, perhaps due to shyness. Since she had never spontaneously wanted to perform a drama with me, I was interested in the fact that she volunteered. In such cases, there may be something that the child really wants to express. In the beginning of a drama, she said that she did not want to go to school because other students were absent because they had colds.

Mother:	If the school is closed due to an infectious disease, you may be absent from school. But now, you are fine, so you have to go to school.
C:	*(In a gentle way)* I won't. *(After thinking a little, she suddenly took something fictional from the side of a chair and pretended to tear it up with a large gesture.)*

Mother:	*(I immediately realized that it was a textbook and spoke in a slightly reproving tone.)* You shouldn't tear up a textbook.
Audience:	*(Laughing together.)*
C:	*(Gaining momentum from the laughter of the audience, she tore up textbooks one after another. While tearing them up with a laugh, she studied my reaction.)*
One of the audience members:	I know. That's a true story!
	(This was important information! I thought that if it was a true story, the act of tearing up textbooks must be some sort of emotional outlet for her. So I smiled and continued.)
Mother:	It seems like fun to tear up textbooks. You look like you're enjoying it.
C:	*(Smiling)* That's right.
Mother:	How many books did you tear up?
C:	Five books, including notebooks.
Mother:	Really? Then I'll try, too. Alright, let's go!
C:	*(She gave me textbooks one after another.)*
Mother:	Oh, it's fun! I feel good! Sometimes it's good to do this. I had a little quarrel with my hubby and felt frustrated. *(I pretended to tear up the textbooks that were handed to me and threw them into the air.)*
C:	*(Looking at me happily)* I can't study anymore because my textbooks have been lost.
Mother:	That's right. You don't have to go to school this semester anymore.

The drama ended there with my remark. Someone in the audience shouted: "It's a great victory!" On hearing that, **C** raised her hands high in the air and went back to her seat in the audience, saying with a smile, "Victory! Victory!"

At a post-class meeting, the homeroom teacher told me that he had never heard that **C** had torn up her textbooks. Meanwhile, when he had met **C**'s mother recently, he heard that **C**'s mother tended to nag at **C** the most because **C** is her eldest daughter. I imagined that **C** always played the role of the eldest daughter and was unable to talk back to her mother or fully release her stress even if she felt pressure from her mother. Tearing up textbooks may have been one of the few ways for her to release stress, even though she did so unintentionally. If **C**'s mother found out about it, **C** would surely have been scolded. So, if she were scolded for having torn up her textbooks in a fictional drama too, she would just experience the same side of her real mother and find no escape from her. In this case, I mirrored her behavior of tearing up her textbooks, accepting her as a person, without scolding her as the mother in the drama.

I performed this drama with **C** in the very early days when I began to practice drama therapy and before I established the IDAM. Since then, I have gradually deepened my analysis through the process of considering how I reacted to children semi-unconsciously. Here is an explanation for this case, drawing on my reflections at that time.

When **C** tore up her textbooks, why did I decide to tear up textbooks with her, even though there were various possible ways to react? I could have said, "Why did you tear up your textbooks? Are you unhappy with something? Tell me anything you like." However, this would be far from the mirroring through which I imitate children's behavior and feelings as their reflection. In the case of **C**, she took such an action because she was unable to verbally express her feelings. It means that even if I had asked her to tell me the reason, that would not have worked. I asked myself why I instantly decided to tear up textbooks. At the beginning of the drama, she said only one thing: "I won't (go to school)." Then she immediately took the action of tearing up her textbooks without saying anything. It seemed that she was not good at communicating verbally compared to the other children in the same scene who rebelled against me and made many excuses. In addition, she had a shy nature, and it was the first opportunity for her to voluntarily participate in a drama. In such a case, I believe that it was ideal that I had accepted her physical communication through mirroring as the mother in the drama. The act of tearing (breaking) something can be said to be a typical way to relieve stress. Moreover, I imagine that she could have achieved catharsis by seeing her mother enjoying tearing up textbooks, not by doing so herself.

When hearing one of the audience members and **C** say "victory" at the end of the drama, I was a bit surprised because I did not have in mind the idea of "winning" or "losing" in a parent-child drama. However, on second thought, I understood that for children, conflict with their mother was a sort of battle and that for children who were likely to be defeated by their mother, the scene that **C** played meant a great victory for them. After the last session, the homeroom teacher asked the children to write a letter to me. **C** wrote that she was happy to have won a victory over her mother for the first time. I realized that it was the first time that **C** had ever won a victory in her battles against her mother.

In that IDAM scene, almost all children rebelled against me, giving a reason not to go to school. I strongly felt that their rebellion was a rebellion for rebellion's sake. This can be seen from the fact that none of the children who played that scene disliked going to school or studying.

"I enjoyed your sessions very much. Through your sessions, I have become free from stress." N.N.

"Your sessions were a lot of fun. I enjoyed dancing and thought about the feelings of other people. I liked the mother-child dramas the most. They were good because I was able to relieve my stress even if I felt stressed by being scolded all the time by my mother." T.T.

Many children gave me such impressions. I thought it good for children to play a role of "authority" and sometimes had them play a role of mother, with me or the classroom teacher taking the role of a child. The following impression was given by one of them who had played that role.

"I had the most fun when I played the scene in which I scolded a person who was just playing and not studying. The reason is that such a scene seems to be common and that I have actually experienced it. I am always scolded at home, but it was fun to play the role of a person who scolds someone." M.A.

Johnson (2021) presents "reversibility" as one of the key components of the playspace. "In real space, authority relations are given little room to shift. One does not playfully reverse roles with one's boss. . . . one needs to act in deference to the authority within carefully prescribed boundaries" (p. 132). The role of the child to be scolded was of course played by the therapist, me. Once in a while I asked a homeroom teacher to play that role. It goes without saying that children enjoyed such dramas to their hearts' content.

Going on a date at a barber shop!?

It is difficult to instantly discover the symbolic meaning of an improvisational drama performed by a child and interpret what significance and effect the drama had on the child. Even if a drama does not seem to be going well, a good process may be going on in the child. Or, as the therapist repeatedly examines what happened in the drama, it is not uncommon that they may gain a better understanding of it later. For these reasons, it is essential for the therapist to continue to examine dramas without giving up when they do not understand them well. It is also effective to review dramas after a while and receive feedback from the perspective of others.

If there is a topic in a class that needs to be dealt with, it is possible to perform a drama other than a mother-child drama. In these dramas, too, the stance of the therapist remains the same in terms of acceptance and mirroring. In one class, I set up a scene of dating at the request of the homeroom teacher. After I decided to play the role of an elementary school girl, I asked the children if someone wanted to play opposite me. Then several boys volunteered. All of them performed a heartwarming drama such as going to Disneyland for a date, and we all enjoyed their performances. However, **D**, who was the last performer, wanted to go to a barber shop for a date. Although I thought that it was a strange date, I followed him. At the barber shop, he wanted to cut my hair and shaved my head, so it was completely bald. I was unable to understand at all why that would happen on a date. His way of talking was obviously strange, artificial, and creepy. At the same time, I felt him releasing a large amount of strong negative energy. I also felt as if he had no regard for others and did not worry at all about what others thought of him.

During a session, I always live on three levels at the same time: (1) as myself, (2) as an opposite player, and (3) as a drama therapist. In each situation, I instantly come up with feelings and thoughts from these three perspectives. At this time, I was in the following states.

(1) As myself: I felt very uncomfortable, receiving his negative energy directly. Although I did not know at the time whether **D** usually talked like that, I felt a considerable threat from his aura and his act of completely shaving my head. I wondered if he was expressing his rebellion against something or if that was his own initiation to the "teacher" whom he had met for the first time. I wanted to say, "When people go on a date, they don't usually take a girl to a barber shop and shave her head. Let's go to a different place. I also want you to speak in a more normal voice."

(2) As the role of his girlfriend: I felt like shouting at him: "Why have you done this? It's incredible you shaved my head. I'm a girl! And I hate the way you talk!"

(3) As a drama therapist: I naturally chose to accept **D**'s behavior and attitude as they were (that is, **D** himself at that time) without knowing why he did so. I acted like I was staring into a hand mirror to check my

new hairstyle. I said brightly and joyfully: "Wow, this hairstyle is cool! I like it. Thank you!" Then he gave me a smile.

The real reason why he shaved my head

In a review meeting after the session, I heard from the homeroom teacher that **D**'s father had suffered severe burns all over his body in a major work accident and that his father always wears a wig or cap because his hair no longer grows. According to the teacher, his father had to undergo dozens of major surgeries and was repeatedly hospitalized. This placed an enormous psychological burden on his mother. Since she had to take care of not only her husband but also her children, **D** and his younger brothers, she was in a terrible emotional state at that time. This solved the mystery of why he shaved my head in the drama. I was relieved to find it appropriate that I accepted him as a whole and was pleased to have my head shaved. Although we happened to go to a barber shop for a date on that day, **D** may have shaved the head of an opposite player in any situation. Later, I knew that his father was in most acute pain both physically and mentally, enough to resent the fact that his life had been saved and that he struggled fiercely for life together with his family members. In addition, the accident happened right in front of **D** and his mother, and his mother clung to him, just a young boy, saying, "**D**, oh, what should we do! What should we do!" According to the teacher, when **D** saw his father, changed beyond recognition from injury, he prayed to God to save his father and thought that if his father went to heaven, he would go together with him. In addition to an unimaginable trauma in his young heart, he must have been very worried about his parents. However, I could well understand that he had to act as a reliable son for his mother and as a reliable brother for his younger brothers at home, and that he had no opportunity to properly express his worry and anxiety.

Accepting an incomprehensible drama

It was in this scene in which I went on a date at a barber shop with **D** that I experienced the importance of acceptance in an improvisational drama with my body and soul for the first time. The fact that he expressed his problem in the drama could have made him feel more at ease. What was even better for him was that I accepted my shaved head, which symbolized his anxiety and worry.

From the following session, his insolent attitude and strange way of talking disappeared completely. Subsequently, I conducted eight sessions in this class. **D** actively participated in dramas in each session, and I always just got the impression that he was a good boy who was good at acting. Regarding my sessions, he wrote in his impressions as follows, "Your sessions were so much fun. Thanks to them, I was able to have a fun experience at school although I thought school was a place to study. I loved your sessions very much."

Emunah (2020) notes that "One objective in the development of a scene is to uncover its symbolic meaning. . . . Such scenes often begin with the client playing a particular role in an *Impromptu*" (p. 129). It is the core element of IDAM and one of the most important jobs of a therapist to discern and discover the meaning of a scene performed by children and encourage them to develop their conscious and unconscious intention.

2. FOSTERING IMAGINATION, CREATIVITY, AND IMPROVING SELF-ESTEEM

Needless to say, imagination and creativity are important and necessary for us. They are abilities, among others, that I want children to improve. I believe that the fundamental energy that creates creativity is imagination. To give just one example, the Wright brothers saw birds flying in the sky and imagined how wonderful it would be if humans could fly. Their imagination led to the creation of an airplane. In other words, creativity that creates new things begins with imagination. In Japanese, the terms "creativity" and "imagination" are pronounced the same, and it is hard for me to believe that this is a coincidence. Drama is one of the best ways to bring out and foster imagination. Moreover, it is one of the objectives of drama therapy to help children use their imagination positively (for instance, in order to improve their lifestyle, heal their heart, and help them realize their dreams).

Wishes to "Jizo"

Since a guided imagery in which participants imagine themselves becoming a Jizo is very effective, I definitely implement this for all groups. In Japan, "Jizo has been worshiped as a guardian buddha of children since ancient times, and people widely prayed to Jizo for providence and salvation of their children" (Mochizuki, 2000, p. 19). Since it often appears in Japanese folk tales, its existence is familiar to many people even if they do not believe in Buddhism. Since children also accept its existence, I conduct this work as a way to have children discover how to realize their wishes and resolve their problems. In designing this work, I was inspired by a workshop organized by an artist of Japanese traditional arts. I have incorporated it into sessions for adults as well as children.

The method is as follows. First, the children close their eyes in a relaxed position. After telling them that they are going to a fun, imaginary world, I say in a calm and cheerful voice, "You are walking through the scenery of a peaceful Japanese village rich in nature." I then ask what they can see, what sounds they can hear, what kind of smells they can catch, and other similar questions. While carefully observing whether the children have gone into their imaginary world in a relaxed and safe manner, I say, "Jizo is standing over there. Let's get closer. [After a while] When I slap my hands together once quietly, you will become Jizo." At this moment, the facial expressions and postures of the children change, with their eyes closed, to those of Jizo. I can see that they are immersed in their imaginary world. There are no children who have not shown any changes. (However, abused children often cannot use their imagination immediately and do not show changes in their facial expressions.) I continue to say, "Now, you are Jizo. Oh, someone is coming to you from over there to make some wishes. What kind of person is it? Listen to the person's problems and give an answer." After spending some time observing the children, I instruct them to come back to the classroom, open their eyes slowly, and return to their original selves. Then I say, "What kind of scene did you imagine? Is there someone who wants to play the scene with me?" Usually, many children volunteer to do so. I ask them to come closer one by one and ask, in a whisper, who came to Jizo, what Jizo answered, and which role the relevant child wants to play in the drama—the person who makes a wish or Jizo. A child's imagination (creativity) is wonderful! In their imagination, various people appear, including an old woman who wants to cure her grandchild's illness, a person who brings a bag and wants to increase the money in it, a child who has no friends and wants to find some friends, and a man who was laid off and wants to find a new job. In their imagination, most of the children fulfill the person's wishes as Jizo. Although there are some mean children (Jizo) who reject the person's wishes, I perform a drama with them according to their stories. Here are some creative interactions.

Young man:	I'm in trouble because I don't have any money.
Jizo:	You can use all the money in this box people donated for me to buy a lottery ticket.

Old man:	Wow, I'm so old, but I still want to get married.
Jizo:	There is a person who loves you at this address: 6–99, 3-chome.
Girl:	I'm very hungry. There's a fork in the road ahead. Which one should I take to get delicious food?
Jizo:	If you go to the right, you'll find a soba and udon shop, and if you go to the left, you'll find a ramen shop or a Chinese noodle shop. My recommendation is the ramen shop.
Girl:	I'll take an entrance exam next year. Which junior high school can I enter?
Jizo:	Judging from your academic ability, you can enter XX junior high school (actual school name).
Young woman:	I want to fall in love.
Jizo:	You can. Thank you for always coming to clean this place. As a token of my gratitude, I'll tell you something good. Go see Mr. XX (the name of the homeroom teacher), your classmate in elementary school.

"You can ride a Nozomi bullet train to your heart's content!"

In a fifth-grade class, I set up a scene in which a mother brings a snack to her child who is in their room after school. **E**, who had been diagnosed with Asperger's syndrome, volunteered to perform a drama.

I started the drama by knocking on the door of the child's room.

Mother:	**E**, I've brought you a cake. May I come in?
E:	I don't want any snacks or cake! (*Although he speaks rebelliously, he is smiling happily.*) (*I decided to eat a cake with him and spoke to him again, completely mirroring his mood and way of talking.*)
Mother:	Don't you want to eat a cake?
E:	I don't care. (*He said in an apathetic but pleasant mood, which went over well with the audience*)
Mother:	(*Similarly in an apathetic mood but with a smile*) I won't give you a cake if you don't care. What do you want to do? Will you eat a cake with me?
E:	I don't want to eat with you. I'll eat alone with the door closed!

Mother:	It's sad that I can't eat with my son. *(I told him my thoughts and left the room, leaving the cake there, according to his request.)*
E:	*(Instantly)* Roar! *(He ate the cake with one bite like a lion, and the drama ended there. The audience laughed a lot.)*

Throughout the drama, he kept moving with dizzying speed while bending his body backward, suddenly screaming and jumping, and running around. I reacted to him while mirroring him with a cake in my hand. I moved so hard that I was almost out of breath. It seemed on the surface that he was releasing a lot of excess energy and some messages. However, it did not seem to me that his inner feelings actually reached the others. The story of the drama and the conversation between us made sense, and both he and his classmates enjoyed it, so it was successful in that respect. However, I did not feel that I was able to truly communicate with him in the drama. One of the main reasons was that he seldom made eye contact with me. I felt that his emotions and energy were circulating inside him, in contrast to his exaggerated movements and voice. It was very tiring for me to act in tune with his energy. This made me realize how tired he was all the time. Anyway, he was able to voluntarily perform a drama with me in front of his classmates, and the drama was accepted with laughter by both himself and his classmates. This must have provided **E** with a feeling of success and confidence in expressing himself. In the following session as well, **E** immediately volunteered to perform a drama. He played the role of a child who refused to go to school in the morning. In the drama, he seemed to be in a bad mood with few smiles. Since he was constantly moving around in the same way as last time, the story did not move forward smoothly. However, he kept performing the drama and did not look like he wanted to stop playing. I patiently continued to react to him for some time. Then, he said, "I want to be absent from school and go buy a model train today." I had known that he loved trains and had a good knowledge of them.

So, I went to a store with him and bought a plastic model of a famous Japanese limited express train for him. I brought the drama to an end there.

After the drama was over, I conducted a Jizo drama, involving all the children. Following my instructions, they closed their eyes, stayed still, and concentrated on their imaginary world. Although **E** sometimes opened his eyes a little and moved his limbs slightly, he kept lying down quietly on the chairs connected to each other. The homeroom teacher was astonished to see him. It seemed to be the first time that he had seen **E** stay still without moving. When it was time to perform a drama, **E** volunteered again. In his story, a boy prayed to Jizo and made a wish that he could ride a 700 series Nozomi bullet train, and Jizo said, "I will grant your wish. You can ride a Nozomi bullet train to your heart's content."

Although Jizo is not familiar in the everyday life of modern children, they can accept the existence of Jizo smoothly. I feel that this is because there is an existence like Jizo in the Japanese collective consciousness and such an existence will surface if appropriately guided. In many cases, children imagine and play a scene in which they can easily project their wishes and have their wishes granted. **E** quietly entered into his imaginary world and proactively created a drama with me. This fact made me feel that drama therapy had served as a trigger to awaken his untapped potential. In his case, it was Jizo that made it possible.

"Bring my husband back to life!"

The following is a Jizo drama that I performed with **F**. He was one of the regulars who volunteered every time to perform a drama with me. Since he always behaved aggressively in the dramas, I was concerned about him from the first session.

His Jizo story was that an old woman was very sad and asked him to bring back her dead husband from heaven. Since he wanted to play the role of Jizo, I played the old woman. "My dearest O-Jizo-san, I've lost my husband, and I'm deeply sad. I want to see my husband! Please bring him back from heaven," I bowed my head in prayer. Then, **F** said, "All right. I'll bring him back to you." It was the first time that I saw him behave calmly. When Jizo brought her husband (the homeroom teacher played this role) from heaven, I as the old woman was delighted with tears in my eyes and said, "Thank you very much, O-Jizo-san! I'm very happy." In that moment, **F** appeared expressionless. However, it was enough for me to see his non-aggressive behavior for the first time. He seemed to feel slightly bewildered and unable to react but remained expressionless when he heard the sincere words of thanks from the old woman. In this connection, Mochizuki (2000), who is a Buddhist priest as well as an art history researcher, describes that "Jizo is a buddha who will save a deceased person who has gone to a faraway place which its family cannot reach" (p. 36). By this token, this drama should be gratifying not only to the old woman but also to the soul of her husband in heaven.

Later, I heard from the homeroom teacher that **F**'s grandfather had died recently. I told him that at **F**'s house, it was highly likely that his grandmother was really sad and wished to see her husband. The teacher said, "Yes, that's right. I think **F** felt good by performing the drama. After the session, he helped me bring a CD player to the classroom although he had never given such help before."

It is thought that **F** gained a feeling of capability and satisfaction by fulfilling his grandmother's wish in the drama, thereby feeling that he could help others. He did not appear to behave aggressively in the drama like he usually did because he was serving as a bodhisattva and was able to be kind to the old woman (his grandmother in real life). It is also important to note that he received sincere thanks from the old woman in the drama. He probably felt good in the drama and, as a result, was motivated for the first time to willingly help the teacher in real life. Though it is impossible to bring his grandfather back to life, he would be able to do a favor for his grandmother in another way after returning home. He "created" a drama from his "imagination" and consequently "created" a new behavior. He was able to learn through experience that it makes him feel good to be kind to others.

Drama makes it easier to transform the "imagination" of children to their "creativity," and it is what children spontaneously want to happen.

"I liked your sessions very much, especially when I entered into my imaginary world. When I imagine something before sleeping, it appears in my dreams, although my classmates do not know this. Thank you for telling me what is very good for me!!" R.Y.

Self-efficacy

I will briefly introduce the concept of "self-efficacy," which Bandura (1997) proposed in his social learning theory and explain the approach of improvisational drama from this concept. In behavioral expectations, an efficacy expectation is defined as the conviction that one can successfully execute the behavior required to produce an outcome, and the efficacy expectations perceived by an individual is called self-efficacy. People who have a strong sense of efficacy deploy their attention and effort to the demands of the situation and are spurred by obstacles to greater effort. By contrast, individuals with low self-efficacy tend to believe that things are tougher than they really are and take inappropriate precautions. This creates stress and a narrow vision of how best to go about solving the problem.

According to Bandura, self-efficacy is based on four major sources of information: performance accomplishments (mastery experiences), vicarious experiences (observing other people successfully completing a task, etc.), verbal persuasion (suggestion, self-instruction, etc.), and physiological and affective states (internal reaction, etc.). It is clear from the research that these sources of information are effective in transforming self-efficacy, that the transformation of self-efficacy leads to the transformation of behavioral performance, and that self-efficacy transformed in one situation is generalized to other similar situations.

It is probable that **F**'s self-esteem improved because he was appreciated for helping the old woman in the drama. Drama enables "performance accomplishments (mastery experiences)," one of the four sources of information proposed by Bandura, and often has the same effect as the actual experience. It is also suggested that similar effects are brought about for other children watching a drama as the audience through "vicarious experiences (observing other people successfully completing a task, etc.)." Since it is obvious that self-efficacy that has transformed in one situation is generalized to other similar situations, it is quite possible that the good results obtained from such a drama will lead to the improvement of other behaviors. This is what must have happened in **F**'s case.

When the child is able to feel that all of themself, including their shortcomings, are recognized and accepted in a drama, it helps them gain a feeling of satisfaction and success, resulting in an improvement in their self-esteem and self-efficacy. This approach is particularly benefiting children with insufficient self-esteem and self-efficacy.

3. REALIZING WHAT PARTICIPANTS CANNOT DO IN REAL LIFE

As you can see from the example of children's dramas after the earthquake mentioned earlier, if you guide children to realize that they could do anything, which they cannot do in real life, within the safe framework of a fictional drama, it often happens that their feelings are healed and their symptoms improve. Children usually resolve their concerns and fulfill their hopes in their dreams and fantasies. However, doing so in an embodied drama has a stronger impact on their real life. There are two main types of dramas in which participants realize what they cannot do in real life: dramas whose world should be brought back to real life, and dramas whose world should not be brought back to real life and should be settled within a session.

(1) Dramas whose world should be brought back to real life

These are dramas that have the effect of making children incorporate the content of a drama into real life or making them transform their real life.

A drama can be used as a rehearsal for real life for such purposes as changing participants' weak points, being able to do and say what they cannot in real life and acquiring a new role or behavioral pattern. Unlike image training in which participants just imagine in their head, dramas require participants to act, using their body and words, to embody their imagination, which brings even more powerful effects.

"I want to quarrel with my mom!"

In a second-grade class, I set up a scene in which a mother tells her child to do their homework. Children actively volunteered, and all of them refused to do their homework. After the session, the homeroom teacher told me that even children who did not actively express their thoughts in regular classes and who could not talk back to their mothers at home strongly rebelled in the drama. Among them was **G**, whose rebelliousness seemed particularly fierce. We quarreled with each other for a while, saying things such as, "Do your homework!" "No!" Then she suddenly shouted at me, "Go away and just take care of my little sister!" This made me realize with a start that she actually had a younger sister and was deprived of her mother's care. While mirroring her anger (with reduced emotional intensity), I made an excuse as a mother, "You are older than your sister, so it can't be helped if I take care more of her." "I don't think so!" she said angrily with serious eyes. I clearly realized that she was living her real life through the drama. After quarrelling some more, we ended the scene. Immediately after the drama, I asked **G** whether she quarreled with her mother at home like in the drama. She answered: "No. My mom always goes somewhere without saying anything."

Immediate effect of IDAM that healed **G**

Later I heard from the homeroom teacher that **G** actually had a younger sister and always had to be a good girl at home without saying what she really wanted to say to her mother. The teacher also said that the girl just happened to be at school on the day of the session although she tended to refuse to attend school in those days due to her defiance of her mother. Her message that seemed coming from her heart told me that she wanted to talk more with her own mother even if she quarreled with her, and that she wanted her mother to listen more to her and pay more attention to her. Although I kept playing the role of an ordinary mother who told her child to study harder, I continued to communicate with **G** by quarrelling with her instead of "going somewhere without saying anything" like her own mother. Perhaps she had a feeling of being recognized by having a chance to make complaints and to be heard. Moreover, she did not have to be a good girl in front of the mother in the drama. She was able to feel refreshed by stopping being a good girl and unleashing her accumulated frustration against her mother (her rebellious energy was strong anyway). Above all, the experience of success and the feeling of accomplishment in the drama as a rehearsal for real life made her feel that she could say what she wanted to say. It is thought that this worked well on a real stage. When I visited the school for the following session, the teacher told me that she was no longer absent from school.

She stopped refusing to attend school. The teacher guessed that this is because the reason for her school avoidance was that she was unable to assert herself to her mother and that the child became able to express her feelings at home.

Usually, there is a counselor at school. However, since counseling is basically conducted verbally, it sometimes takes a great deal of time to identify the causes of problems and resolve them only through talking. Even if a counselor talks to **G**, an eight-year-old girl, I am wondering if she can say that she rebels against her mother by refusing to attend school because she is angry with her mother, who takes care only of her younger sister these days. It is almost impossible for children at these ages to verbalize what is happening in their mind or even to be conscious of it.

Meanwhile, in the drama, she said, "Go away and just take care of my little sister!" Drama can clarify such important information in a moment. Improvisational dramas not only make it possible to obtain such necessary information immediately but can also sometimes bring about desirable transformations to a player in a short period of time. For the child who had to take on the role of the eldest daughter and be a good girl for her mother, it was necessary for her to verbalize her accumulated anger and defiance of her mother. In addition, she needed to externalize these feelings vocally and to enjoy the successful experience of having been able to rebel against her mother. Her case is a good example of how performing a drama, rather than just talking with a counselor, can produce great results when it is used properly with good timing. This drama with **G** was the starting point for me to create IDAM. The changes that occurred in **G** were dramatic and very straightforward. This function of drama therapy as training for role acquisition is very important. Participants can acquire a role and character that they do not have (but want to have) by practicing playing such a role and character.

This is a good example of a drama whose world should be brought back to real life.

According to Bandura's theory mentioned above, **G** attained physiological and affective states and performance accomplishments (mastery experiences) by saying what she wanted to say to her mother in the drama, increasing her efficacy expectation that she could say what she wanted to say to her mother in real life. Moreover, according to the homeroom teacher, she became able to communicate better with her classmates after the drama, which led to the resolution of her friendship issues. This is also a good example in the sense that it shows that self-efficacy transformed in one situation is generalized to other similar situations. In this way, IDAM improves the quality of life of children.

I have also often received reports from adult clients, stating that they realized their dreams like they did in the drama. They say that the real feelings and satisfaction that they experienced in the drama gave them the energy to be positive in their lives and the power to realize their dreams. It can be said that the difference between reality and drama is very thin, sometimes paper thin. Acting by using your body, voice, and feelings makes you feel that you have had a real experience where you fulfilled your dreams and desires and can convey to the brain almost the same feeling as when you actually did so. Even if it is impossible to realize your dreams and desires in real life, a successful experience in a drama produces a good feeling and has a positive impact on you, and this remains in your body and brain to give you power in real life. You do not escape from real life to the fictional world of drama but bring back the achievements and fun that you experienced in a drama to real life. Van der Kolk (2015) writes, introducing the study of Damasio and his colleagues, "[R]ecalling an emotional event from the past causes us to actually reexperience the visceral sensations felt during the original event" (p. 95). In other words, the brain cannot tell the difference between something we imagine and something that happens to us in real life. Just imagining eating a lemon makes you salivate, which is one of the familiar examples to demonstrate the above function.

The only thing to remember is that to experience this sense of realism and satisfaction, the drama must be based on the absolute condition that a reliable therapist or peer sincerely cooperates with and watches over the drama. If a drama develops only with superficial conversation, at the worst it may bring about an unpleasant feeling. Needless to say, it is important for a drama therapist to create mutual interaction and a sense of unity among participants while gradually proceeding with the drama process.

The dramas mentioned above provide the opportunity for participants to rehearse what is feasible in real life. Meanwhile, there are other dramas that enable participants to achieve their impossible dreams and desires, such as seeing someone whom they will never see again, just like **F** "bringing the dead grandfather back to life."

(2) Dramas whose world should not be brought back to real life

These are dramas that deal with negative desires and should be settled within a session. When participants want to do something that generally seems bad or unforgivable, or when they want to experience something that is not realistic, it is important that they relieve stress and fulfill their desires only in a drama. If you can do something negative in a drama, such as defeating someone who treats you badly, you will be able to refresh your mind and body. If these desires are achieved in a drama with the support of a receptive therapist and group members, the negative energy is often alleviated. This often happens in adults, and in the case of children, it happens very dramatically and immediately in many cases. However, the most important thing to keep in mind is to have participants distinguish between drama and reality and prevent them from bringing the world of a drama back to real life.

When children try to do something bad in a drama, you have to be careful that the drama will not serve as a rehearsal for real life. You should judge the degree of danger, and if you allow the scenario to proceed, you should fully contain and resolve their feelings in the drama. An extreme example is the act of murder. The following is the case of **H**, in which you can see how **H**'s drama was brought to a closure.

"Let's kill the neighbors!"

H, a fifth grader, actively participated in IDAM in each session. The following is a scene in which a mother brings a snack to her child who is in their room after school.

(The mother knocked, entered **H***'s room, and saw* **H** *holding something like a big gun at the window and shooting it with the sound "Bang! Bang!")*

Mother:	What are you doing?
H:	I'm shooting missiles.
Mother:	How did you get such a dangerous thing?

H:	I bought it.
Mother:	Please let me see it. (*I received the gun from him.*) What's this? Is it a real gun?
H:	(*Calmly*) It's real. I was fighting and killing people in a neighbor's house.
Mother:	Were you fighting people in a neighbor's house? Why? Did they do something you didn't like?
H:	No. (*After clearly denying it*) I'd just like to do that. *I decided to mirror his behavior. This is because the fact that his classmates watching the drama kept laughing from the beginning greatly helped create an atmosphere of a fun play. Accepting his behavior meant that I accepted himself existing in front of me at that moment. In addition, by doing the same thing as him, I intended to further amplify his feelings and make him express them, and as a result, sublimate his aggression in a fun framework with my support and that of his classmates.*
Mother:	Well, the wife in that house is very spiteful, and I don't like her. Let's do it together! (*We set up a chair inside the window, from which we fired at random together, saying: "Here we go. Rat-a-tat-tat!"* **H** *looked very happy with this extraordinary reaction of his mother and the action that we took together. After shooting, I pointed out the window and spoke to* **H**.)
Mother:	Look!
H:	(*After looking out the window, he looked back at his mother*) Everyone is dead.
Mother:	We did it. (*While saying this, I shook hands with* **H**.) I am so surprised. Anyway, let's eat sweets and calm down. (*We ate sweets, smiling awkwardly. This went over very well with the audience.*)

If such an act is witnessed by adults, such as parents and teachers, even in the middle of play, they are very likely to say, "You shouldn't kill people in the neighbor's house." At least the odds of "killing" people together with an adult would be quite low. **H** looked very happy. Although it is important to determine how you should react, taking into account the conditions and symptoms of the relevant child, the framework of a drama makes it possible to accept the child's feelings and express empathy for them even in such a situation. It can be said that the setting of an unrealistic and extreme scene like this makes the drama even more fictional. In the subsequent session as well, **H** set up a similar scene and expressed his aggression. Since three sessions were scheduled, I decided to tell him by the end of the third session that he was allowed to act aggressively only in a drama and that he had to resolve his aggressive feelings when the session was over. This is because "derolement" from an aggressive character in a drama is indispensable. During a drama in the final session, I created a mood in which I was partly the mother and partly my real self, and talked to him with a smile: "**H**, you've been addicted to fighting recently, haven't you? I'm worried about you, so please stop it." "OK," he said obediently and played a scene in which he put water in a bucket, placed it on the floor, and washed his feet in it. He then smiled at me. ("Washing one's feet," in Japanese culture means to quit doing evil deeds.) I was touched to hear his inner voice symbolically through this behavior. "Oh, yeah. That's fine," I praised him as both a mother in the drama and a therapist.

How wonderful children's creativity is! If children are contained within the safe framework of a fictional drama, they express, sublimate, and resolve their negative feelings, as seen in the case of **H**, who showed me in a literally dramatic way that he understood what I had said. In other words, as Hartley et al. (1952) states, "By permitting the child to play freely in a setting of security and acceptance, we enable him to deal satisfactorily and healthfully with his most urgent problems" (p. 17).

I should note here that it is completely unrealistic and fictional for a child to use a real gun in a neighborhood or school in Japan. If children under the burden of the gun culture, for instance in the United States, would play a similar scene, it would surely develop to be creative and surprising, due to children's spontaneity and imagination, such as the school was filled with supermen so nobody got hurt, or all the bullets were chocolate marbles and children loved them.

It is thought that in a drama, adults and especially children find it easy to do (or say) what they cannot usually do (or say) and can heal themselves if they are able to do so. I have received many impressions as shown below.

"Your sessions were always fun. Since I was able to express my thoughts clearly, I was really looking forward to your sessions. It was a little embarrassing for me to perform the drama, but I was very happy when I expressed my thoughts. Although I was unable to say them to my classmates, I was delighted to be able to clearly express my thoughts in the drama." H.S.

"I'm glad that I was able to think and talk about my feelings that I had been unable to express before. Your sessions were very fun for me. I enjoyed the dramas the most because we were able to do what we wanted." Y.Y.

It is critically important that children have everything accepted in a drama, including what is generally considered unfavorable, as well as their negative feelings, which often tend to be denied. Some of you may find it difficult to accept everything in all cases. However, it can be relatively easily done in the safe framework of a drama.

4. EXPERIENCING EMPATHY WITH PEERS AND A PLEASANT SENSE OF UNITY

School avoidance and suicide caused by bullying at school go beyond the scope of serious educational issues and are serious social issues. If drama therapy, as introduced in this book, is offered in the social groups of children (schools and other groups), where they spend most of their time and energy, it can provide the opportunity for them to share their feelings with their trusted peers. It is very significant for them to experience empathy and a sense of unity among themselves. Since there are complex factors behind these problems, it may be difficult to find drastic solutions immediately. However, if individual members of a school or group can connect emotionally with each other, this may lead to resolution on a much larger scale, as when individual cells of the body become healthy, which in turn affects the body as a whole. Although the family is the most representative social group to which children belong, the family has recently been losing its original function, and more incidents have been occurring at home. In recent years, the increased number of cases of domestic abuse has been reported in Japan since the COVID-19 pandemic. Although it is important to take countermeasures against this problem, what is just as important is that schools and other social groups to which children belong outside the home need to play a crucial role. Drama therapy provides the opportunity to identify dangerous situations for children and help maintain and restore their health and enables both individual and collective transformation.

"Drama therapy gave me the opportunity to interact and play with my classmates. Since I didn't have many such opportunities, it gave me a good experience. Due to drama therapy, I can now talk to those I don't usually talk with. That's why I have become friends with many classmates.

Since there were only three of your sessions, I cherished each one. I will never forget the memories of drama therapy." Y.K.

5. IDAM AS A "HEALING DRAMA"

Kawai (1987, p. 64) calls as a "healing drama" a drama that has an important meaning in the process of play therapy. According to him, the features of a "healing drama" are that the emotional expressions and performances of the child are truthful and that the script and direction of the drama are owned by the child, while the therapist just follows the directions of the child. He cited an example of some play therapists in which such a drama appeared after therapy being provided more than 20 times. In IDAM, however, I note that such a "healing drama" appears in a drama of only a few minutes in length even in sessions that are conducted only a few times (or once in some cases). There are many cases in which even if a scene appears to be simple and light-hearted on the surface, it has deep meaning or leads to significant healing for the relevant child. To name a few, these cases include such dramas as **A** got to the toilet in time, **G** quarreled with the mother (after that, she did not miss school anymore), **I** ate steak worth one million dollars, and **K** prayed to Jizo for peace. (See Chapter Four for cases of **I** and **K**.)

Why can a "healing drama," which Kawai denotes, emerge even if sessions are conducted only a few times? Why can healing occur during such a short drama? The reason lies in the unique structure and form of IDAM, as described in Chapter Two. One of the major reasons is that the therapist actually lives together with the child in the drama. Another factor is that the therapist deeply introspects each drama after it ends. As a result of introspection, a therapist understands the meaning of the dramas performed by children. And, in proportion to the depth of the therapist's understanding the children do heal and recover themselves. By sincerely seeing through dramas and deeply understanding them, a therapist will be able to bring about change and recovery to clients even if the number of therapy sessions is small. Furthermore, there may be related the instinctive power of children with problems and concerns. Murase (2009), a Japanese psychotherapist, notes that "seriously ill patients and child patients truly capture the therapist's comprehension even if their other functions are impaired or underdeveloped." I also agree that children have such acute sensibility.

Additionally, the audience as co-creators play another major role in IDAM. The quality of the drama space with an audience is completely different from when the same drama is performed in a therapy room with only two people. The audience and the space on the spot protect children performing a drama as a container, as witnesses. Even in situations where children spill out their negative feelings, the presence of an audience softens their feelings and helps prevent them from becoming too serious. The audience unconsciously plays the role of a brake, giving a performer aesthetic distance. It seems to me that the presence of an audience works to encompass potential pathology in children. In most cases, on the contrary, children can perform a drama in a very good mood, drawing much laughter. What is required of the therapist is to bring playfulness to a group and a space. Children performing a drama can gain confidence by being supported and well received by the audience. The audience also receives a good stimulus. Once children begin to realize that a drama space is a safe and fun space in which they are accepted, the space is increasingly matured and enhanced each time a child performs a drama. With these processes may arise a situation where the most therapeutic moment appears in a drama in succession, even from the first drama.

I have an interesting thought that children who I feel may have deeper concerns and problems, judging by their responses in games and their drama content in IDAM, enjoy drama therapy more deeply than other children. I always direct my attention to such children in the first session. There were such children in every class. Although I did not do anything special for them, but treated them equally with the other children, it was obvious that they enjoyed IDAM more deeply than others. I learned this from their letters of impressions as they wrote more words of gratitude to me there. It is as if ointment applied to the chapped skin penetrates into the chapped part of the skin more deeply than into the healthy part. Meanwhile, ointment applied to the healthy part of the skin can help prevent the healthy skin from becoming chapped in the near future and keep the entire skin healthier. That is to say, in terms of the prevention and early detection of mental problems and proactive mental health care, IDAM can be said to be an effective means even for children who may not need therapy right now.

Therapist's Solution of "Conflicts" and Child's Power to Heal Themself

Four

In the previous chapter, I explained how children healed themselves while enjoying a drama by presenting some specific scripts. All of the cases introduced were successful. Even if children rebelled against me at first, the dramas were satisfactorily settled on the spot or our conflict was resolved.

On the other hand, there are some cases in which things do not go that easily. In the early days when I began to practice IDAM, there occurred three dramas in a row in a fifth-grade class, where children became aggressive. My usual interaction with them through acceptance and mirroring did not yield fruitful development and rather produced drama scenes difficult for me to handle, of which I could not readily find a way out. This kind of deadlock inevitably occurs in therapy. Needless to say, children do not hate therapists. They just transfer their feelings that they have for a certain person to a therapist in a drama. However, even experts who are familiar with this may feel uncomfortable when negative feelings are directed at them by a client in any type of psychotherapy. It is necessary for therapists to repeatedly overcome such a deadlock and cultivate their knowledge and skills.

In this chapter, I will present processes of two types of cases: one is the case of the boy **I** diagnosed with ADHD, which worked very well by my accepting the child's words and storylines, and the others are the three cases of the boys **J**, **K**, and **L**, all of whom were considered to have "no problem" by the homeroom teacher. The dramas with them did not seem to work well at all, which resulted in my experiencing uncomfortable feelings. These feelings raised a question in me how children would be feeling about their own dramas. By analyzing the trajectories with the four children, I gained deep insight on the four main reasons of the therapist's discomfort:

1. The story does not follow the "four-part organization" of Japanese narratives, i.e., beginning, development, turn, and ending, and lacks meaningful progression.

DOI: 10.4324/9781003565062-5

2. The three children cannot stay in dramatic reality from the perspective of Pendzik's 6-Key assessment.
3. The conflict continued with children in rebellious characters.
4. Actual physical violence was used as part of a play against the therapist.

I will discuss them more in detail later in this chapter, following the scripts of these dramas.

Despite these shortcomings of uncomfortable dramas, these dramas, in which children were not responding in the way the therapist expects them to respond, turned out to be necessary and significant for these children, and I discovered the underlying meanings of these dramas through quite impressive reconciliation I had with them after and outside of these dramas.

I will also explain a simple way to evaluate whether or not children have the power to heal themselves. Let us first look at the dramas of creative storyline with the boy **I**.

1. TREASURE OF ONE MILLION DOLLARS

Before I conduct the first session, I always ask the homeroom teacher to tell me any information that I should know in advance, such as situations children have with particular problems or about whom the teacher is worried. The teacher of this class said that the only student she was worried about was **I**. He was diagnosed with ADHD and was seeing a psychiatrist regularly and taking medication. According to the teacher, **I** sometimes went out of the classroom to go to the dispensary or lay down in the corridor while thrashing his legs about. She told me that it was good that he was trying to control his bad feelings like this without taking it out on others. She also asked me to be aware that **I** might leave the classroom suddenly.

During a game that I conducted at the beginning of the first session, when I asked if there was someone with high stress levels, **I** answered, "That's me." His answer impressed me. After that, I conducted a game in which I acted out various feelings and had the children guess what kind of feeling I had acted out. We then played the game One Hundred Faces with "Ah". **I** voluntarily came next to me to hold my hand. After the performances of several other children, **I** expressed his state of mind with "Ah." **I** lay on his back in the middle of the circle, while thrashing his legs about, and shouted "Ah!!!" as if he were spitting out his frustrated and powerful energy. He showed little facial expression.

I felt that he was filled with stress. When all of us mirrored his "Ah!!!", he laughed happily. After some other children performed, **I** volunteered again and repeated almost the same "Ah!!!" All of us imitated it again. He looked happy, in high spirits. No matter how many times a child makes the same expression, I accept it and never say that it was the same as before. I then instruct other children to sincerely imitate the whole movement. If a child makes the same expression over and over again, they are doing that because they need to do so. In this game, everyone mirrors the expression of a performer all together. This enables the performer: (1) to feel they have taken the lead, (2) to feel everyone understands their feelings, and (3) to feel everyone accepts them. They will feel even more so if their feelings are negative. The game also helps create a sense of unity and empathy among those who mirror the expression, and even children who do not have the courage or energy to do something alone can enjoy doing this, feeling that they can do anything if they can do it with others. It is one of the best introduction games because it can produce a lot of laughter.

When I later watched the video taken at that time, **I** was touching me and attaching his body to mine in a casual and natural way. When I conducted the same game in the second session, I did not sense his frustrated energy like last time. In addition, he had more expression in his voice and on his face than last time. The camera had captured his smile at that time, which made him look extremely happy.

According to DSM-5 (2013, pp. 59–60), the main symptoms of ADHD are (1) inattention (absent-mindedness, poor attention/concentration span), and (2) hyperactivity (being unable to stay still, constantly moving about) and impulsivity (acting on sudden urges, losing one's temper easily). **I** watched the dramas performed by me and his classmates as part of the audience without moving around and concentrated on and enjoyed all the games and dramas without leaving the classroom. In my sessions, he showed few signs of inattention and hyperactivity. Regarding impulsivity, he was suddenly excited only once in a drama scene as shown below. Although I was a little surprised at the sudden outburst, I did not feel it was too strange because it is quite normal for something extraordinary to happen in a drama. This is because I tell the children in advance that they are free to do anything they want in the dramas, and also because the program is designed to allow them to freely release their feelings. I also purposely encourage them to express themselves through my receptive attitude.

"Mom, go to the hospital!"

The following is the IDAM scene that **I** and I performed.

In the afternoon, after a child has returned from school, his mother knocks and enters the child's room.

Mother: (*With a happy voice*) I've brought a snack for you. What were you doing?

I: I was drawing a picture.

Mother: What were you drawing?

(***I*** *walked quickly to the blackboard and drew something like a big robot. To the left of it, he drew something like a dwarf who was very small compared to the robot and put a speech balloon near the mouth of the dwarf, in which he wrote "Help!" I was surprised that he suddenly came to the point and, at the same time, felt that the robot represented his mother and that the dwarf, who had asked for help, was himself.*)

Mother: What is this? Is this a robot?

I: No, this is a monster! This is a human, and he says, "Help!"

Mother: Hmm. This is a monster, not a robot. The human next to the monster says, "Help!"

[*I just repeated what he said.*]

I: (*His attitude changed suddenly. He stamped his feet, while shaking both his hands up and down, and screamed at me loudly and very hysterically.*)

Mom has a split personality!! Mom is ill, so go to the hospital!!

Mother: (*In a calm tone, I confirmed this with him firmly.*) Wait a second. Do I have a split personality?

I: Yes!! Go to the hospital!! (*He was excited and kept shouting.*)

Mother: I got it. I haven't noticed it myself. Hey, **I,** sometimes I say to you, "(*Mirroring* ***I*** *and in a hysterical tone like him*) **I**, go and study!!" and other times I say to you: "(*Smiling in a gentle tone*) Hey, honey, won't you have some snacks?" Is this right?

I: That's right!! (*He remained in a state of excitement.*)

Mother: (*Accepting the fact*) Well, I have a split personality . . . (*suddenly understanding*) All right! I'm going to the hospital now! I'll have my split personality cured at the hospital. **I**, wait in your room and eat your snack. See you later. Bye!

When I went out waving my hand, he suddenly calmed down from his excitement and smiled very happily. Since I acted in a lighthearted manner as if I were going to a nearby convenience store to have my split personality cured (creating such a lighthearted atmosphere also helps emphasize the fictional drama mode), the whole drama had a comical and fun atmosphere. This went over very well with the audience, bringing laughter, which made **I** feel happy.

Later, I heard from the homeroom teacher (who heard from **I**'s mother) that when **I** was scolded by his mother at home, he was depressed and stayed in his room until her mood calmed down, and after coming out of his room, he talked to her as if nothing had happened. I judged that **I** probably did not scream at his mother hysterically in his real life like he did in the drama and that he stayed in his room, feeling depressed and screaming in his heart, "Help!" until his mother's anger subsided. He may have spilled out his inner thoughts that he himself was not ill, although he saw a psychiatrist regularly, but it was his mother who was ill and needed to have her illness cured at the hospital. I fully understand how happy he felt seeing me going to the hospital in the drama. In this drama, he had the experience of having his feelings of frustration and his thought that his mother, not he, was ill being accepted probably for the first time, and fulfilled his desire to have her illness cured at the hospital. On that day, he wrote the following impressions:

> "When I performed a drama for the first time, I had a lot of fun. When my classmates performed a drama first, I enjoyed it very much. Then, I thought I'd give it a try. So I volunteered. After a while, I was finally selected and performed a drama. Everyone laughed to see my drama. I think that was very good. Drama therapy makes me forget the passage of time. I'm grateful to you. Thank you very much."

He was probably not aware of what the mother-child drama that he created on the spot meant and of why he felt happy enough to forget the passage of time by performing the drama with me. However, the fact that the drama went over very well with his classmates made him think that it was very good. Performing the drama was of great significance for him. It is said that many people with ADHD have lower self-esteem or self-efficacy (Rickel & Brown, 2007). It may have given him confidence and triggered a change in the image that his classmates had of him. For instance, it was possible that the image of him had changed from a strange guy who sometimes went out of class to a guy who created an interesting drama and was a good performer. This would lead to a transformation of the group as a whole.

When I visited the class for the third and final session, **I** began quarreling with his classmates as soon as the session started. He was scolded by the homeroom teacher and began to get cranky. The teacher soon took him out into the corridor so as not to disturb my session. During a break, I went out into the corridor and talked to him. However, it did not seem that his good humor would be restored immediately. Since I had heard from the teacher that his psychiatrist had given him stronger medication than last time and the side effects put him into a slight daze, I did not strongly encourage him to participate in the session. I just expressed my regret and left him to the teacher. He was unable to attend the session until the end.

When I was talking with the principal in his office after the session, the homeroom teacher came to say, "**I** is pestering me to give him a chance to perform a drama with you, Ms. Onoe. He says that otherwise, he won't go home. So I need some help." He was crying in the middle of the stairs. The area around the chest of his T-shirt was soaked with tears. I decided to perform a drama with him. Since he agreed that the teacher would join us as the audience, the three of us entered the classroom. I asked him what kind of drama he wanted to perform. He said it was the mother-child drama that his classmates had performed on that day.

"Let's eat steak together!"

Mother: **I**, you'll be late for school. Go at once!

I: No.

Mother: Why?

I: My whole body hurts. (*He seemed to be frustrated and rebellious against me.*)

Mother: Well, are you sore all over? Then, you may be absent from school. (*I immediately accepted the fact that he did not want to go to school and that his whole body hurt.*) I have to call your teacher.

I: Tell the teacher that you have run away from home.

Mother: Then, I can't call your teacher. **I**, do it yourself.

I: (*Although he seemed a little uncomfortable, he understood what I meant and called his teacher reluctantly.*) Hello.

Teacher: (*The teacher pretended to pick up a phone receiver at the desk where she sat a short distance from us.*) Hello. Ah, **I**, it's you. What's wrong?

I: Well, my mom has run away from home, so I'll be absent from school today.

Teacher: Oh, boy! Your mom has run away from home. I see. You're going to look for her, aren't you? Take care.

I: OK. See you. (*He hung up.*)

Mother: What did she say?

I: She said she didn't like you. (*I found that he wanted to remain rebellious against his mother and draw her attention to him by saying something mean.*)

Mother: What? Did she say that? Wow, I'm shocked. I like her, but she doesn't like me.

Anyway, **I**, you are sore all over, aren't you? I'll give you a massage. Poor boy! I wonder why your whole body hurts. Where does it hurt? (*I massaged the part of the body that he said hurt, such as the back and shoulders, while talking to him in a gentle manner.*)

I: (*Suddenly*) Do you want to know the truth?

Mother: Yeah. Tell me.

I: The truth is that the teacher said she liked you.

(*This shows that* **I** *has a straightforward personality. Since his "mother" gave him a massage out of concern for him, his rebellious and nasty feelings disappeared.*)

Mother: Really? I'm glad to hear that. **I**, do you love me?

I: Yes. (*I loves his mother in real life, not me.*)

Mother: Wow, that's good! I love you, too! (*By saying so, I gave him the message that his mother in real life loves him.*) Hey, did your pain go away?

I: Yes. But the area around the waist still hurts.

Mother: I see. Then, how about lying down?

I: OK. (*He lay on his stomach on the floor.*)

Mother: (*While having a similar conversation, I sincerely massaged the parts of the body that he said hurt. Although I knew that he actually did not have any pain in his body, I continued to enthusiastically give him a massage for a few minutes, praying that my massage would heal his emotional pain. Since I was not used to doing so, my hands later became hot and sore.*)

I: (*While receiving the massage, he suddenly picked up a small piece of trash that had fallen onto the floor.*) Hey, I found something amazing!

Mother: What? What is it?

I: A very old treasure! A very valuable one! (*It seemed that his imagination and creativity began to work probably because he felt satisfied and relaxed by receiving enough care.*)

Mother: Wow, great! **I**, you've found such a great thing! Let's display it at home as a family treasure! (*I tried to receive it from him.*)

I: We should exchange it for money, instead of saving it. This is worth one million dollars.

Mother: One million dollars!! Whew! We should exchange it for money, shouldn't we? Then, I'll sell it right away for cash. Do you want to buy something with that money?

I: Steak.

Mother: All right, steak. I'll buy some meat and cook a steak for dinner. (*I quickly played the scene alone in which I exchanged it for money, bought steak, and returned home.*) I've bought some steak. **I**, let's eat steak together!

I: (*He stayed lying down.*) Aren't you going to cook the steak?

Mother: (*I was surprised to hear this because I intended to go on to the next scene, omitting the scene of cooking the steak. The scene in which his mother cooked was important to him.*) Oh, I'm sorry. (*After playing the scene of cooking in the kitchen.*) **I**, dinner's ready!

I: (*He stood up and sat at the table.*)

Mother: Hey, look! It's amazing. It looks yummy. This is top-quality Matsusaka beef. I'll cut it for you. I'm cutting it into ten pieces, so each piece is worth 100,000 dollars!! Savor it well. Shall I feed you?

I: Yes.

Mother: Open your mouth. Ahhh!

I: (*He opened his mouth and let me feed him obediently.*) It's yummy! *Although for a fifth grader, he was in a state of regression, I worked hard to mother him by showing affection and indulging him as much as possible within the framework of the drama.*

Mother: Good! Please feed me, too! (*I opened my mouth and had him feed me.*) It's yummy! I'm happy to eat steak with you. So, this is the end of our drama!

Although the drama developed in an unexpected way due to his great idea, it goes without saying that we were able to end the drama in a good mood. To my surprise, he returned to his "normal" self after the drama ended, and politely bowed to me and said, "Thank you very much." He looked much more mature than the boy who had behaved with me like a small child just now. He then went back to the classroom to get ready to go home. When I returned to the principal's office and resumed conversation with the principal, **I**, who was ready to go home, came to the glass door of the principal's office and waved at me.

Afterward, in a meeting to review the session, I heard from the homeroom teacher that it had been true that **I** was absent from school due to body pain. According to the teacher, one day, he went to his mother's bedroom and asked to sleep together with her. After his request was refused, he slept on the floor near her bed all night. When he got up the following morning, he felt painful all over and was absent from school. I think the fact that he was refused by his mother was a very shocking incident for him. It was found that he had expressed his unfulfilled feelings and had had the experience of observing the "atonement" of his mother in the drama. I strongly felt as the mother in the drama that he loves his mother very much. By playing opposite a client in a drama, you can directly receive and understand their feelings that you cannot know by only objectively directing the drama.

"When will you come next time?"

After my three sessions finished, I received impressions from all of the children who participated, which were written in the form of a letter. The following is **I**'s letter:

> "Hello, Ms. Onoe. How are you? I'm fine. Thank you very much for your sessions. At the time of the third session, I was sulky and cried the whole time without attending it. But my teacher brought you to me, and I was able to receive drama therapy. I was very happy with it. I will never forget you. I am truly grateful to you. Thank you very much."

About three months later, when I visited the elementary school to conduct a session in another class, I happened to see **I** after school. We noticed each other at the same time. He rushed to me and we held our hands. Since **I** and I had spent time together performing a drama with deep meaning, our hearts instantly resonated at that moment, re-experiencing the mood of healing that we had shared three months before. He looked much happier and healthier than when I saw him before. The first thing he said was, "When will you come next time?" While I was taking out my notebook to see my schedule, he wore a smile and said in an adult-like tone, "I'm sorry [for bothering you]." After hearing the day of my next visit, he went home cheerfully while repeating the date many times. Although he did not tell me directly in words that he wanted to see me again, I understood his feelings. After all, it was the last time I saw him. Later on that day, the homeroom teacher told me that he was recently in good condition and was no longer taking medication. The teacher also said, "Since he has been in a good mood recently when coming to school in the morning, his mother is likely doing her best to see him off to school at least." Although I do not usually have the opportunity to meet the children involved again after finishing my sessions, it was a re-encounter brought about by chance. Given the teacher's report that suggested that the relationship between him and his mother in real life had improved, it may have been an inevitable opportunity caused by his desire to thank me again.

I received the following question from a trainee who listened to this case: "In the drama, he was able to feel happy and satisfy his unfulfilled feelings by creating a good relationship with 'his mother,' which he could not build in real life and by telling 'his mother' what he could not say in real life. Such a positive experience in the drama is different from his real experience. Accordingly, when he confronts his mother in real life, doesn't it happen that he is disappointed with the difference between drama and real life or rather feels depressed?"

This idea overlooks the fact that what he experienced in the drama has brought about significant changes in his inner self. Children feel great satisfaction by expressing their feelings, attitudes, and thoughts in a drama which they have suppressed or have been forced to suppress and by being accepted, receiving care and affection from "a mother." They actually feel with their whole body and heart in dramatic reality. The feeling of release that occurs at that moment unleashes some kind of taboo sealed inside of them. This sense of being liberated allows them to experience another world almost instantly and changes their inner self.

This also brings about changes in the recognition of themselves, their mother, and the relationship between them. Even when they see their mother in real life, such changes remain in their body and heart. Through a drama, children unconsciously change their feelings, attitudes, and responses toward their mother in real life, and their mother also feels these subtle changes. I believe that this mutual interaction (mothers and children become each other's mirror) create a relationship different from before. Although it varies depending on each case how a new relationship is actually built, it is a natural result that if a person who has received therapy has changed, this also results in changing a person who has not received therapy.

In the case of **I**, the feedback provided later by the homeroom teacher traces the change that enabled him (and perhaps his mother) to respond better to reality. It is of great and profound significance that children feel satisfaction to the fullest even in a drama.

2. THREE UNCOMFORTABLE DRAMAS WITH A "CONFLICT"

I will describe the dramas with the three boys in the same class as **I**.

The importance of two perspectives

The three dramas based on *my memory and impression* were uncomfortable as the children kept a negative attitude against the mother. This was my subjective feeling that I directly felt when playing opposite them. After a while, I was given a video taken by the homeroom teacher and watched the dramas objectively like one of the audience. I was surprised that the two impressions were so different that it is better to say that I was shocked rather than surprised. The latter gave me the impression that the boys simply enjoyed performing a drama, sometimes acting playfully.

This experience made me acutely aware that it was necessary and important for a therapist to not only act in a drama and understand a client's raw feelings as the second party but also watch the drama objectively from outside as a third party. I am absolutely convinced that consideration and analysis of a drama from both of these perspectives would lead to better interventions and therapeutic outcomes. What surprised me more were the letters from the children who participated in the first and second sessions. Although I was afraid that the relevant three children had not enjoyed their dramas, I was surprised to know that they, just like all the other children, had enjoyed themselves very much and that they were grateful to me.

The need for a therapist's self-reflection

In these cases, it is very important to check whether I projected my personal feelings evoked by countertransference because the discomfort that I felt during and after the dramas in which I played opposite them cannot be just my groundless imagination, and thus cannot be ignored.

My supervisor, Sally Bailey, told me that only I knew the answer as to whether I had projected my problems. She also said, "If so, you should admit the fact and learn from it. From then on, try as much as possible to face the moment of therapy with the best consciousness and concentration." I seriously thought with both head and heart about whether I had any personal feelings from the past that were dragging me down. Consequently, I reached the conclusion that this was not the case, and I had been doing my job properly as a drama therapist, focusing my concentration on the spot at the moment, with the utmost priority placed on my intent and desire to make the children feel good.

Thus, I was able to learn with *a real experience* that facing myself with humility is important for my growth as a therapist.

In counseling, the transference or countertransference of feelings is useful for therapeutic purposes in many cases. In IDAM, however, since we basically aim to achieve healing in a short improvisational drama performed only once or twice, personal negative feelings of the therapists must be well controlled by all means. Even if a client transfers their negative feelings onto a therapist, the therapist must not be affected by these feelings in the drama, in order to implement this approach effectively.

Yet, I wanted to understand and verbalize what it meant if I felt such feelings although I had no problem on my side. Accordingly, I closely watched the video over and over again to examine in more detail what happened in the dramas and made many discoveries. After some consideration, I thought that if I sensed the children's negative feelings during the dramas while *playing opposite them, the feelings that I received were their true feelings* even if objectively they seemed to enjoy performing the dramas or if they pretended to act playfully. I clearly realized this obvious fact from the bottom of my heart. The truth comes out even if the performers just play their role in the fictional framework and setting of a drama, or it comes out all the more in the drama. I can feel their raw feeling flow into my body and soul in a drama. Again, the performers feel uncomfortable or healed even in the fictional setting of a drama because the drama deals with their real feelings under the disguise of the role of someone else. That is the essence of drama therapy.

At this time, I reconfirmed that IDAM, in which a drama therapist plays opposite a client, is a serious match that requires the therapist to concentrate heart and soul. No matter how short a drama is, or just because a drama is very short, I should not dare to take it lightly. I was struck anew with the awesomeness of drama.

Next, I will specifically review each drama while showing my thought processes and what I felt about the children during the dramas.

Drama 1: "You killed my dad with a knife, right?"

J:	*(Digging something with a shovel at the edge of the stage, seemingly in the garden at home.)*
Mother:	It's time to go. Otherwise, you'll be late for school. Go at once.
J:	I don't have to go. I'm digging. *(He digs up a ball about the size of a basketball and slippers from under the ground. They were actual things that happened to be there.)*
Mother:	Wow, you found various things! *(I accepted the fact that he wanted to dig up something and what he dug up.)* But you'll be late for school, so go at once.
J:	*(Continued digging all the time.)* I won't go because I've burnt everything, including my correspondence notebook, textbooks, school bag, and other things.
Mother:	*(I did not act like I was angry at him but like I was taking the situation seriously.)* Did you burn them all? I have to call your teacher. *(I pretended to pick up a phone receiver and said in a very embarrassed manner.)* Hello. This is the mother of **J**. Well, my son said he had burnt his textbooks. So I'll let him skip school today.
	The homeroom teacher, who participated in the session, joined the drama on the spot and answered the phone from her seat in the audience and told me in a surprised manner.
Homeroom teacher:	Oh, is that so?
	*Although **J** kept digging something in the corner of the stage, he eventually threw the ball and slippers that he had just dug up at me when I was talking on the phone. I pushed them aside with my hand and made an angry face at him, gesturing for him to stop, while talking with the teacher in a good temper as if nothing was happening. Since I acted this a little comically and in an exaggerated way, the audience laughed, which served as motivation for him to throw more at me. However, it did not seem to me that he wanted to attack me, but rather, he was just enjoying acting playfully a little too much.*

J: *(Beginning to strike together two pieces of wood, which happened to be there, like clappers. This made the audience laugh.)*

Teacher: *(Hearing the commotion)* What's going on? Is there any problem?

Mother: *(Trying to be cool)* No. Well, our dog is making a noise. *(Both the audience and* ***J*** *laughed.)*

J: *(He threw the ball at me again.)*

Teacher: *(Amiably)* Don't worry about textbooks. He can share textbooks with the person next to him. Please, tell him to come to school. *(The teacher had understood what I explained about IDAM and participated in the drama as a good assistant.)*

Mother: All right. I haven't talked much with him yet, so please don't scold him.

Teacher: No. I promise.

Mother: *(After hanging up, I adopted a serious and angry attitude as the mother in the drama.)* **J**, come on!

Although he was digging near the edge of the stage, he ran off the stage to the edge of the classroom while holding the two pieces of wood. As a mother, I wanted to talk with him properly in his room (on the stage) and continue the drama physically in the center of the stage. I tried to bring him back to the stage, pulling his hand.

Mother: Come here!

J: You're abusing me. You're going to kill me!

Mother: *(Suggesting the fact that he threw things at me many times)* Who is abusing whom?

(Although ***J*** *barely returned to the edge of the stage, he did not come any further. I gave up bringing him closer and sat alone in the center of the stage. We talked to each other from a distance.)*

J: *(He dropped to his knee, adopted a fighting pose, and raised his right hand high while holding clappers in both hands in some kind of martial arts posture)* Come on!

Mother: *(Quietly)* Why did you throw things at me when I was talking seriously on the phone?

J: Yesterday you killed my dad with a knife, right? *(Sudden information!)*

Mother: *(Although I did not know what he meant, I accepted his scenario.)* I didn't kill him. *(I tentatively denied it.)*

J: *(In an attitude like a detective in a TV drama)* The investigation has already been completed! *(The audience laughed.)*

Mother: Oh, I admit I quarreled with him yesterday. But I didn't kill him!

(If the investigation had been completed, I should have admitted what I did. However, since murder is an extreme act, I admitted that I had committed just a minor sin.)

J: You killed him and then ate him!

The audience laughed. Since the audience sometimes laughed, the drama seemed to be developing in an easy-going and playful atmosphere. He seemed to be half-serious and half-joking. Although he had a smile on his face, his attitude toward me remained unchanged. He kept his fighting pose. As the mother I wanted to talk with him about his textbooks and school but his responses to me completely missed the point. I felt it was impossible to continue to talk with him about school. I thought that if I did not fight against him, his feelings would not subside. So I mirrored his pose.)

Mother: Then, I'll accept your challenge!

J: *(Jumping on this chance, he adopted an attitude like a samurai who was about to fight. He said in a slightly thick and low voice)* I've practiced kendo. I can't afford to lose to you!

Mother: *(While mirroring his mood and way of talking, I consciously adopted an exaggerated attitude and way of talking to keep our emotional distance so that his feelings would not become too strong.)* I used to practice kendo, too. I can't afford to lose to you!

J: No way! You're lying! *(Imitating my mood, he said in an exaggerated and theatrical way.)*

Mother: I'm not lying!

J: I guess you quit kendo as you were clumsy!

Mother: You've inherited your clumsiness from me!

J: No!

We stayed in the same place without moving at all and had this exchange in a loud voice, while keeping the same distance and taking a fighting pose using both hands. After he shouted his denial to what I said, his tension was getting too intense. Feeling that his energy and spirit were about to reach the limit, I suddenly relaxed in order to ease his tension and returned to the usual way of talking and the usual voice and volume as a mother.

Mother: It's true I used to practice kendo.

J: *(He looked slightly relieved and unconsciously mirrored my usual way of talking. He said in a childish and obedient way.)* Really? I'm suspicious. *(The audience laughed.)*

When the atmosphere eased, one of the audience members complained, "This drama is a little long. Why don't you finish it soon?"

The audience became a little noisy. Although I ignored it, he immediately stopped brandishing the two pieces of wood and lowered his hands as if he was affected by the words of his classmates.

J: My arms have become stiff, so let's stop.

It seemed that he said this as the character in the drama, and at the same time, it seemed that he intended to bring the drama to an end as his real self. Anyway, I returned to my real self and laughed. However, he then hid behind the two pieces of wood, using them like shields, and took a defensive posture with his face emerging from between them. For him, the drama was not yet over. I also did not want to end it halfway. Although he had a superficial smile on his face in a playful way, he kept me away physically. He dodged my stroke with the wooden shields and protected himself with them. Although it seemed that he was protecting himself from being scolded by his mother, his attitude showed that even if she stopped scolding him and tried to hug him with love, he would not easily accept her. To get out of this dead-end-like situation, I tried expressing a new feeling of sadness.

Mother: I'm sad to hear you say something strange to me. *(He showed no change. So changing to a reassuring way of saying.)* **J**, listen to me. The teacher said you could share textbooks with the person next to you. So, go to school!

J:	I've burnt my school, too. It no longer exists. *(No matter what I said, he rebelled against me in that way for a while. He was keeping the same posture.)*
Mother:	Are you going to keep fighting with me like this?
J:	Yes.
Mother:	Do you want to fight with me?
J:	Yes.
Mother:	Do you like fighting?
J:	Yes. This is my revenge against you!
Mother:	*(I was surprised to find that he wanted "revenge". I did not know whether he wanted revenge due to his mother's attitude or on behalf of his father. So, I just repeated his words.)* This is your revenge, is it? This is your revenge against everything I've done, is it?
J:	You killed my friend, too. *(Although I denied that I had killed his father, he said that I had killed his friend, "too." This meant that he still believed that I had killed his father.)*
Mother:	*(I thought that it was high time to apologize to him.)* I am a bad person, right? I've done a lot of bad things. I'm sorry I haven't noticed.
J:	*(There was no sign that he would stop fighting. He did not seem to be satisfied with the apology. Quite the contrary, it seemed that he was not moved at all.)* Such flattery doesn't work on me!
Mother:	It's not flattery.
J:	*(Abruptly he went out of the classroom and immediately opened the door to come in. He returned to his real self.)* We can stop the drama here.

I did not know whether he was worried that the drama was getting too long out of regard for his classmates, or if he really wanted to stop the drama. I felt that I should not end it until he made up with his mother. The first thing that I needed to do then was to derole him, even just as a matter of form. So I said to him half as the mother in the drama and half as my real self, extending my hand, "Let's make up." *Since he took the defensive posture again, using two pieces of wood as shields, I said that the drama was over. His classmates also said the same thing, and he finally shook hands with me. He then swirled our hands in the air. To an outside observer, it seemed that he got a little playful. However, when I carefully watched this scene in the video, I found that he was still rebelling against me and was not reconciled with me at all. Though I managed to bring an end to the drama, I heard the cry of his heart. While swirling his arm around, he was crying,* "I'm not shaking hands! This isn't a reconciliation! I'm angry. I don't forgive you!"

To my surprise, the title of **J**'s impression on that day was "A letter of Gratitude."

"A letter of Gratitude for Drama Therapy: Thank you very much for your session on Friday. I'm sad that the next session will be your last. . . . Please, do not make the next session the last one and come again. I particularly enjoyed the dramas. I was looking forward to them every time. I'm excited about what we will do next time."

Although I asked the homeroom teacher for information on **J**, there was no particular information other than the fact that he was "an ordinary child."

Drama 2: "You threw away my toy, right?"

Mother: It's time to go. Otherwise, you'll be late for school. Go at once.

K: (*In a rather relaxed way*) Wait. I'm now playing with Wazatora-man (*The name of a character that a boy who performed a drama a few turns earlier than* **K** *had come up with on the spot and was well received by his classmates. Its Japanese connotation is an "artificial superhero," here its miniature.*)

Mother: Put Wazatora-man aside and go to school at once. Do you have your correspondence notebook with you?

K: I mistakenly threw it away in a garbage truck instead of putting it in my locker. (*He was not rebellious but was just telling this fact to his mother.*)

Mother: In a garbage truck? Well, what are you going to do? What should we do?

(I did not say this in an angry way but rather wonderingly. He also seemed to be wondering together with me. I did not blame him and spoke gently.) Shall I tell your teacher about this?

K: *(After thinking for a moment, he said quietly.)* Maybe.

Mother: *(I tried to confirm what he wanted to do.)* Shall I call now or go to school with you?

K: Call the teacher.

I talked with the teacher on the phone as in the case of **J** *mentioned above.* **K** *was playing beside me. From his action of slightly tapping my shoulder (although I did not notice it until I watched the video), I gained the impression that he was an obedient and gentle child and felt his love for his mother. The revelation that he loved his mother was a new discovery for me. Although he usually showed no expression and did not smile, he seemed at that time to be playing with peace of mind under the protection of his mother, feeling happy because his mother was worried about him and was talking on the phone for him.*

Mother: *(After hanging up the phone)* The teacher said you can use a substitute notebook. Take this with you. *(Although he was expressionless, he obediently received the substitute notebook from me and was about to go to school. I was relieved to see this.)* Let's play together with Wazatora-man after you come home. OK, good boy! See you later. Take care.

K: *(When I thought that he would go to school without causing any trouble and that the drama with* **K** *would end, he suddenly looked back with an impassive face and spoke with a low, small, and expressionless voice.)* Yesterday, you threw away XX (the name of a certain toy), right?

Mother: *(I wondered if his real mother had thrown away his toy without his permission.)* I haven't thrown it away. Did something go missing?

K: You threw away YY *(another toy)*, right?

Mother: I haven't touched your toys at all. Did something disappear?

He did not answer my questions at all. He just listed the names of various toys, saying, "You threw away ZZ, right?" *I spoke while mirroring his way of talking and facial expression. For instance, when he grinned and told me that I had thrown away his toy, I denied it while grinning in the same way as he did.*

In my memory, this scene was very nasty. However, when I objectively watched the video, he seemed to just act very playfully and did not appear to ignore my questions or rebel against me. This is because the audience sometimes laughed and because I was also grinning, mirroring him. The therapist's intention to conduct marked mirroring is difficult to realize in a real situation. A fictional drama, on the other hand, enables the therapist not only to mirror in an apparently marked manner and often to exaggerate, but also to create even playfulness from the drama itself. If this interaction with him takes place in "reality," I may appear not to be caring for him truthfully but just making fun of him and may possibly hurt his feelings. The drama can easily give performance a sense of humor and elicit laughter from all as they enjoy it.

K: (*Suddenly*) Do you know the voice of Wazatora-man?

Mother: (*Glad that I could finally have a conversation with him and answered his question.*) I don't know. What kind of voice does he have? Try it!

K: (*He did not answer my question and just said the name of a certain toy.*) You threw away AA, right?

Mother: Hey, what kind of voice does Wazatora-man have?

K: You threw away BB, right? (*He relentlessly repeated the same sentence in a monotone voice with flat emotions. I felt that the energy in his voice and body was very low.*)

Mother: (*I tried to defuse the situation.*) It's no good anymore. It looks like my son has lost his mind. (*In a slightly playful way*) Are you okay? (*After placing my hand on his forehead, I moved my forehead close to his—in Japan, a mother often does this when she wants to know her child's temperature. Then, before our foreheads touched, he bashed his forehead against mine.*) Ouch! (*Actually, it hurt very much. He also seemed to feel pain.*) Are you all right? (*I placed my hand on his forehead again.*)

K: Oh, well. I'll go to school. See you later. (*He walked a few steps and looked back.*) You threw away CC, right?

Mother: Are you okay? Take care.

K: (*In a surly tone*) OK. (*While walking, he mumbled with a small voice.*) I'm about to enter a shopping street, so I have to watch out for cars. (*As soon as he said it in a monotone voice, he bumped into a car in front of him (actually, the grand piano located there) and became motionless. It looked like he was dead.*)

Mother: (*I rushed to him.*) Are you all right? (*Since I had thought that the drama was over when he went to school, I did not know what this meant. Thinking that the drama should not end with this ending, I gently tapped his back and said with a big smile in the most playful way as possible.*) Oh, dear! He's dead. Oh, no! My son's dead. (*Immediately, I raised his body, held him in my arms, and laughed.*) It looks like he came back from the dead as Wazatora-man!

K: (*After thinking for a moment*) Roar! (*He obediently came back from the dead according to my words and went back to sit in the audience with a smile.*)

During the drama, I had no time to think why he chose a scenario in which he died in a car accident. What did it mean? In this drama, he listed the names of about 30 toys, asking me if I had thrown them away. His relentless questions made me uncomfortable. In addition, he ignored my own questions, which made a conversation impossible, and bashed his forehead against mine. Because of this, I had a negative interpretation of his "death" at first. I thought that I had lost the opportunity to make up with him and have a meaningful conversation with him, that he had refused to play with Wazatora-man together with me after returning home, and that he had rejected me forever through his death.

However, after many reviews of the video and his impressions, I came to think that he might have been trying to punish himself. In other words, he may have tried to pay for his sins by causing trouble to himself because he made his mother feel pain. This is because when he left home, saying, "Oh well. I'll go to school. See you later," it did not seem like he was attacking his mother. In my impression, he walked unsteadily, feeling sorry for having been unable to respond to his mother's kindness and say nice things, and collided with a car. I realized that he had chosen to kill himself. However, he never did anything bad enough to atone for it with death. Did he get depressed, lose hope and kill himself because a lot of his toys were thrown away? Where did this idea come from? Did he act on the spur of the moment, or was it something he had in his mind that was embodied in the drama?

Although I have experienced many IDAM dramas, including the ones conducted at an orphanage and other facilities, in which the performers killed others, he is the only child who made a scene of his own death. Anyway, it can be seen that **J** expressed his inner self by attacking (blaming) his mother until the end, whereas **K** expressed his inner self by attacking (blaming) himself at the end. It is natural that dramas reflect the differences in each child's condition or situation at that time, their relationship with their mother, and personality.

Takahashi, a psychiatrist, (2016) argues that a person who has not nurtured self-love tends to blame themself and is unable to assert themself to others. He then states that this development of nurturance depends on whether they were accepted by their mother for their self-assertion when they were small. **K** still behaved and uttered in a frail manner, yet repeated the phrase many times, which can be interpreted as his utmost "self-assertion" that he ever tried. His statement of "self-assertion" for so many times on this day might have been elicited because he was accepted by the mother in the drama.

The following are **K**'s impressions.

> "I always look forward to drama therapy sessions. I cannot believe that the next session will be the last one. Each of your sessions has relaxed me. I've incredibly enjoyed your sessions. I will participate in your last session, cherishing every moment of the two hours. Oh, how much I'll miss your sessions after that."

Of all the impressions of the children in this class, his impressions pierced my heart most deeply. I had thought that he did not have a good impression of me because he showed little expression and did not seem relaxed and also because he made me feel pain. Accordingly, I was very surprised to know that he would miss my sessions very much and especially that my sessions relaxed him, and that they were good for him. Although I had thought that I could sensitively appreciate and understand the feelings of others (especially those of clients during sessions) until then, the drama with **K** was a good opportunity for me to realize that I still had a lack of understanding.

After my sessions were over, I heard from the homeroom teacher that **K** had climbed the railing of the outer corridor on the third floor. When his classmates shouted in surprise, a PE teacher happened to pass by and took him down from the railing. The teacher said that although he did not know whether or not **K** just wanted to attract everyone's attention, the slightest mistake could have led to his death. I feel that it is unlikely that what a child expresses in an improvisational drama is completely unfounded. I wonder if death sometimes crossed his mind. Hayashi, a philosopher, (2000) argues that the role of death in a child's world is by far powerful, immediate, and serious than adults may presume, and that the difference between a mimicry of death in a play and an actual act of death is often only a fine line. Anyway, I am very glad that he obediently followed his mother's words in the drama and "came back from the dead" and that he "incredibly enjoyed" my sessions.

Drama 3: "I can't go to school because I have a fever of 50°C (122°F)!"

Mother: It's time to go. Otherwise, you'll be late for school. Go at once.

L: No. (*With a mirthless expression, he made no attempt to move, sitting cross-legged.*)

Mother: Don't say "No." You'll be late for school.

L: I won't go because I lost my correspondence notebook.

Mother: What? (*Many children had used the same excuse so I joke around a little and talk to myself.*) That seems to be popular these days.

L: Call the teacher. (*It seemed that he half asked me to do this and half took it for granted that I would do it.*)

Mother: (*I did not want to follow through right away because I felt that he had just imitated his classmates regarding the correspondence notebook and phone call to his teacher, and that he did not perform his own drama. I wanted him to express himself.*) I'll call the teacher later. Did you look for the notebook everywhere?

L: Yes. I looked for it, but I can't find it. Call the teacher.

Mother: It's embarrassing to call her to talk about this. What should I say?

L: (*With a slightly commanding tone*) Call her!

Mother: I see. I'll call her.

L: (*As soon as I picked up the phone, he immediately brought the ball that* **J** *had used before and began to throw it at me with a big smile, as he had planned from the beginning.*)

Since I have experienced an unpleasant drama three times in a row, I felt more uncomfortable. In the case of **J**, he did not plan to throw the ball at me. That seemed to happen naturally while he was performing the drama. However, in the case of **L**, it seemed obvious that he had planned this "crime" from the beginning. What is more, when I watched the video later, I found that **J** threw the ball at me a little gently, rather taking care that the ball would not directly hit my body, although I did not know this when performing the drama. In contrast, **L** threw the ball hard, directly at me. He seemed satisfied to see me talking with the homeroom teacher on the phone in a cool way as in the case of **J**. With a smile, he seemed amused to see his mother embarrassed at the situation.

Then, he threw the ball toward **J,** *who was then watching the drama as a member of the audience and began to play catch with him. Although I knew that he did so without malice, he went too far with his playful attitude. If this had continued, the drama would have become tedious and lost its meaning. My discomfort increased further.*

My real self: *(I hung up the phone with the homeroom teacher and returned to my real self.)* Hey! Do not go too much away from the play nor involve the audience to do such a thing. If you don't really want to enjoy the drama, I'll end it.

Classmates: No.

My real self: *(Pointing to the stage)* It doesn't matter what happens in a drama. But I won't allow you to do what you did just now! *(It was the first and only time in my three sessions that I clearly showed such a resolute attitude.)*

J: *(With a humble tone,* **J** *spoke from his seat in the audience)* I'm sorry.

L: *(Although he did not say anything, he had the same expression as* **J***.)*

My real self: *(It seemed to me that things had settled down.)* Then I'll resume the drama. *(I quickly returned to my "gentle mother" persona and continued to act.)*

Mother: The teacher said on the phone that you could bring another notebook.

L: I can't go to school because I have a fever. I have a fever of 50°C (122°F).

Mother: *(I accepted the fact that he had a fever of 50°C and placed my hand on his forehead.)* Your forehead is very hot! Go to bed right now. *(I let him lie down on the spot.)* I'll go and get a doctor. *(I showed a very worried attitude.)*

L: There's no need.

Mother: Oh, I'm really worried about you. Here's a cold towel. *(I cooled his forehead with the towel.)*

L: *(He pushed the towel off of his forehead, showing no charm at all.)* I don't need this!

Mother: No. Don't remove the towel. *(I did not react to his non-obedient tone but kept taking good care of him.)*

L: Juice! *(In a commanding tone)*

Mother: *(I acted like I was trying hard to respond to the request of my sick son.)*

You want some juice? All right. *(I hurried up to get some juice.)*

L: *(As soon as I went to get some juice, he got up with a grin and began to play a game in the corner of the room. He looked as if he were laughing at his mother because she was worried about his condition although he just pretended to be sick.)*

Mother: Don't play a game. You have to go to bed. You have a fever, don't you?

(At this point, I had two choices as to how to behave as a mother. One was to realize that he was faking being sick and try to correct him, and the other was to continue to be worried about him. I chose to play the role of a mother who is worried about his health. This is because I felt that he wanted to rebel against his mother and defeat her and because he began to perform his own drama (without imitating his classmates' dramas).)

L: When I measured my temperature a short while ago, I had a fever of 10°C (50°F).

Mother: That can't be true. If you had a fever of 10°C, you'd die. (**L** *and the audience laughed.*) I've brought you some juice.

L: I don't need it! *(He had a great amount of rebellious energy.)*

Mother: I've brought this because you wanted some juice.

L: I want only a cola!

Mother: You said juice.

L: I don't know.

Mother: Hmm, what . . . *(Although I wanted to try to soften the atmosphere by asking what had happened to him, he interrupted me.)*

L: *(He pretended to measure his temperature with a thermometer under his arm.)* Oh, I now have a fever of 0°C (32°F).

Mother: *(It was obvious that he was rebelling for the sake of rebellion. I put a thermometer under his arm.)* You have a fever of 38°C (100°F). What a high fever! *(I cleared my mind and made one more try at suggesting a reconciliation.)* Well, if I bring you a cola, will you drink it and go to bed?

L: No. I'll play a game while drinking the cola.

Mother: *(Since it became difficult to continue to play the role of a mother who was worried about him, I proposed conditions for exchange.)* You can't play a game. You have to take care of yourself. If you promise not to play a game, I'll bring a cola. Then, will you drink it and go to bed?

L: *(After thinking it through)* No.

Mother: Then, I won't bring a cola. *(Softening my tone)* What shall we do?

L: All right. *(I understood that he promised not to play a game. However, while hooking his little finger with mine as the sign of a pledge, he sang the Japanese play song "Yubikiri Genman (pinky promise)".)* Yubikiri genman, if I tell a lie, I'll play a game! *(Originally, the song goes like this: "If I tell a lie, I'll swallow a thousand needles." In English, the following rhyme may be easier to understand: "Cross my heart and hope to die, stick a needle in my eye." Although the lyrics are fairly extreme, it has been traditionally used when we make a promise.)*

Mother: It's different. You have to say that you'll swallow a thousand needles if you tell a lie.

L: *(With the rhyme of "Yubikiri Genman")* No, I won't! *(The audience laughed.)*

Mother: Don't say that. Drink a cola and go to bed.

L: I want a Sprite!

Mother: We have no Sprite at home. *(I became more uncomfortable and had an edgy attitude.)*

L: Then, a cola is okay.

Mother: I see. *(I happily returned to the "gentle mother" persona.)* Here you are. *(I was expecting him to drink the cola and go to bed.)*

L: *(Suddenly using a forceful tone)* I said I wanted some water! *(Things usually do not work that well.)*

Mother: *(As a therapist, I was trying to feel what he wanted to convey. Meanwhile, as the mother in the drama, my patience was nearing its limits. I half talked to myself, like asking myself a question.)* What has happened to **L**? You're always a good boy. I'm a little confused today, so I won't take care of you anymore.

L: All right. I'll play a game. *(He continued to be defiant, and there was nothing charming about his attitude. He received the cola that I brought, soon discarded its contents without drinking any, and returned the empty glass to me.)* I drank it myself.

Mother: Well, you don't need a drink, do you? You don't care if you don't get healthy, do you? *(I felt quite uncomfortable.)*

L: I don't care because I won't go to school. (*After saying that, he looked a little awkward, perhaps thinking that he may have made his mother really angry. I noticed this look on his face when I repeatedly watched the video later. He seemed to think that he had to take some measures. He put the thermometer under his arm and spoke in a slightly childlike tone.*) I'll check my temperature one last time. Wow, 500°C (932°F)! (*The audience laughed. After that, he soon returned to his former attitude.*) Go buy me a Sprite!

Mother: I won't care about you anymore. You don't drink any cola or water I bring.

L: It's already nighttime, so I'm going to sleep. (*He crouched down on the spot. However, he got up immediately after a second, looking as much as if to say that he did not follow his mother's instruction.*) Is it morning already? (*He seemed to want to play the scene of the following morning.*)

Mother: It's nighttime, so you went to sleep. Okay, this is the end.

Many other children who have rebelled against me in a drama have accepted my kindness or stopped rebelling at an earlier stage to somehow agree with me. However, **L** *stubbornly rebelled against me and did not accept me at all. I felt that even if all his unreasonable demands had been physically met, his heart would not have been really fulfilled. I had no choice but to end the drama at that time because I thought that we would just be going over the same ground.*

L: (*Although he had a slightly dissatisfied look, he returned to the audience.*)

The following are **L**'s impressions:

"I experienced drama therapy for the first time, and I enjoyed it very much. What I enjoyed the most is the drama in which a child did not want to go to school in the morning, and the drama of **J** was the most interesting for me. Following this, the drama of **K** was also interesting. My drama did not excite the audience at all, but I enjoyed it."

Although the homeroom teacher said that she had no particular comments to make about **L**, there was one thing I had been concerned about since before I performed the drama with him. At the beginning of the first session, I conducted a game "An imaginary yardstick." When I asked children whether they have a brother or sister and whether they are glad that they were born into their family, **L** came to me at the time of both questions and asked me, "My little brother is dead. How can I answer?" To prevent this from happening, I always ask the homeroom teacher whether there are any children whose parents have divorced or who have lost family members before I think about questions to ask in a game. At this time, however, I had not heard about his younger brother. When I asked the teacher about his younger brother later, she did not know anything about it. She said that it was probable that he died some time ago, given the fact that **L**'s parents did not tell her about it. Anyway, I wanted to avoid a situation in which **L** would be so worried about his brother's death that he could not enjoy the game. I told him to just think about his current family with the intention of lightening the burden on his heart.

At first, I unconsciously had a shortsighted view that if his younger brother was dead, he could receive a great deal of affection from his parents (for his younger brother's sake). Accordingly, this image of being loved by his parents was at odds with his behavior in the drama (he turned his strong rebellious energy against his mother and unreasonably ordered drinks one after another). It is something that I should definitely avoid when doing this job, to imagine such a thing without any evidence. Meanwhile, it is also shortsighted to assume that he is not loved by his parents for the reason that he rebelled against his mother in the drama. I *re-realized* that I should have considered various other possibilities regarding his relationship with his parents in a more flexible manner from the information about his brother's death, regardless of the actual situation of his family. For instance, I could have thought that he felt guilty deep in his heart because he is alive. I could also have thought, as just one example, that he was dissatisfied with his parents' mourning for his deceased brother, wanting them to pay more attention to him who is alive.

3. WHY DID I FEEL UNCOMFORTABLE?

I will discuss here four reasons I have found for these dramas not working well and giving the therapist unidentified discomfort. These phenomena indicate some inner issues children harbor in their mind and are unable to express exactly what they are and appear symbolically as a pointless drama uncomfortable to the therapist. Since these latent troubles present themselves in the structure of dramas and children's performance, the following four reasons will help the therapist understand children and assess a drama more objectively.

Reason (1) No "four-part organization"

There is no "ending"

As a result of watching the video repeatedly, I have realized that the first factor was that the storylines of the three dramas did not follow the "four-part organization" of Japanese narratives which consist of beginning, development, turn, and ending. There were no endings in these dramas. On the other hand, in the case of dramas with other children, I found that no matter how short they were, they always ended with some ending. Interestingly enough, in such dramas, the logical process of introduction, development, turn, and ending appears spontaneously. I will introduce two dramas with **I** as good examples of this.

Drama 1

Introduction: The mother brought a snack to the child's room.

Development: She drew a picture of a monster and a small human on the blackboard.

Turn: He complained that his mother had a split personality.

Ending: She said that she would go to the hospital to get it cured, and the drama concluded happily.

Drama 2

Introduction: **I** said that he would not go to school because his body hurt.

Development: He called the teacher himself.

Turn: While his mother was massaging his back, he found an expensive treasure.

Ending: The mother exchanged it for money, and they ate a steak worth one million dollars together, and the drama ended happily.

Meanwhile, the endings of the dramas with the three boys were completely different.

Drama with J

Introduction: **J** was digging in the garden.

Development: His mother called the teacher because he said that he would not go to school.

Turn: He quarreled with his mother, brandishing two pieces of wood, and continued to take a fighting pose.

Ending: None. (Since he said, "We can stop the drama here," it seemed that he brought the drama to an end. In fact, however, the drama did not come to an end at all. He just interrupted the drama.)

Drama with K

Introduction: **K** said that he had thrown away his correspondence notebook.

Development: His mother called the teacher.

Turn: He continued to pick a quarrel with his mother, saying that she had thrown away his toys.

Ending: (Regardless of the story so far.) He died in a car accident while going to school.

(The drama had no ending about his toys. It was interrupted by him, although there was still a gap in our conversation and hearts.)

Drama with L

Introduction: **L** said that he would not go to school because he lost his correspondence notebook.

Development: His mother called the teacher.

Turn: He continued to order various types of drinks, saying that he had a fever.

Ending: None. (I interrupted the drama because we were never going to reach an ending.)

The four-part organization, originated from Chinese poetry, is generally taught in elementary and high schools in Japan (Sato et al., 2008), and it is unconsciously recognized as a basic premise for narratives by Japanese. However, these three dramas were suddenly interrupted at the third part. Thus, we feel uncomfortable when listening to or performing a story that does not follow this organization. I think my body responded strongly as "not feeling right" and was physiologically uncomfortable. To put it differently, this narrative structure itself is a big part of why IDAM was working with the other children. If you are habituated well with this structure of narratives, you will know when to end the drama by intuition. As shown above, some children can form an ending (or a happy ending) whereas some cannot. Although I always intend to bring the drama to a pleasant ending for the child, ending cannot be consciously produced. I do not impose one that I think is good, of course. I just provide support so that an ending can be spontaneously formed through interaction between the child and me.

There are so many techniques in drama therapy, depending on the population of the therapy and the purpose of the session. For instance, when therapy is provided for the purpose of seeking how to resolve a problem, a therapist often consciously stops the drama in the middle. It is also common for a therapist to dare to try an unpleasant ending so that the participants can learn about human relationships.

Since IDAM is conducted for the purpose of relieving children's stress and healing them, and a drama is only a few minutes long and is performed only once for each child in most sessions, it is important to form an ending. Besides, a happy ending is of great significance from a therapeutic perspective.

Reason (2) Unable to stay in dramatic reality

I figured out that the second factor was the fact that the three children were not able to stay in dramatic reality.

Pendzik (2012) created a qualitative assessment called the 6-Key Model "based on the notion of dramatic reality" (p. 198). She explains that general psychotherapy takes place in the ordinary reality and at a metalevel that includes transference and countertransference contents, but in drama therapy the main processes take place within dramatic reality, and in the transition between dramatic reality and ordinary reality (Pendzik, 2012). Reflecting on the therapy sessions from the perspective of the Keys helps the therapists assess and understand the participants, and the therapy process as well. These are:

> Key One: Passage—Entering and Exiting Dramatic Reality
> Key Two: The Quality or Style of Dramatic Reality
> Key Three: Roles and Characters
> Key Four: Content Patterns—Plots, Themes, Conflicts, and Symbols
> Key Five: The Response to Dramatic Reality from the Outside
> Key Six: The Meta-Reality—The Unmanifested Subtext
>
> (Dickinson & Bailey, 2024, pp. 136–141)

The second reason why I was uncomfortable and felt that the dramas were not going well pertains most aptly to Key One and Two. From the viewpoint of these Keys, **J** and **L** were obviously unable to maintain dramatic reality. They went back and forth between dramatic reality and ordinary reality and were unable to return to ordinary reality smoothly at the end. **J** repeated stopping the drama in the middle, then, resuming it, and going out of the classroom suddenly. **L** started playing catch with **J** in the audience in the middle of the drama.

Huizinga (1964) argued the following in his famous book, *Homo Ludens*:

> Animals play just like men. We have only to watch young dogs to see that all the essentials of human play are present in their merry gambols. They invite one another to play by a certain ceremoniousness of attitude and gesture. They keep to the rule that you shall not bite, or not bite hard, your brother's ear. They pretend to get terribly angry. And—what is most important—in all these doings they plainly experience tremendous fun and enjoyment. (p. 1)

These comments by Huizinga are intriguing when looked at from the perspectives of Key One and Key Two. He suggested that play was perceived as an unreal world with certain rules (even by, or all the more for animals!). The space where animals pretend and play represents the very dramatic space where they enjoy playing as they maintain it. Thus, it is thought that many children unconsciously understand to pretend to do things in dramatic reality and play. However, the fact that two of the children actually threw a ball at me and one child bashed his forehead hard against mine shows that they could not confine their negative feelings in dramatic reality of pretense.

Reason (3) The conflict with children in rebellious characters

Another reason was that the characters children played were all rebellious and conflict with them never ended. Characters and contents of these dramas are what Pendzik's Keys Three and Four evaluate. I will examine these Keys from the lens of *amae*, which Doi (2005) uses to expound and assess human relations in a unique way as follows. He notes that the concept of *amae* is important as an organizing principle in understanding the characteristics of Japanese people, while at the same time he believes that "this concept has a universal applicability inasmuch as the patient's transference can be interpreted in terms of *amae*" (p. 140). He asserts that "though it primarily indicates a content state of mind when one's need for love is reciprocated by another's love, it may also refer to that very need for love because one cannot always count on another's love, much as one would wish to do so." Therefore "*amae* is more keenly felt as a desire in frustration than in fulfilment" (p. 141). He points out that there are three patterns of mental conflict caused by the lack of experience of *amae* as follows:

(1) People cannot *amaeru* even if they want to do so. (They feel that *amae* on the therapist poses a threat to them.)
(2) No matter how much people *amaeru*, they do not feel satisfied. (They try to maintain the relationship of *amae* with the therapist.)
(3) People find themselves without desire to *amaeru* and have a strong sense of distrust. (Although they supposedly have an inner desire to *amaeru*, they avoid facing their desire.)

(Doi, 1961; Yamatake, 2018)

Each pattern seems to apply to the three boys. Pattern 1 is reminiscent of **K**, who said, "You threw away my toy" in a monotone voice without expression and did not establish a conversation. Pattern 2 describes **L**, who kept asking the mother to bring him various drinks. Pattern 3 seems to apply to **J**, who continued to take a fighting pose, saying that the mother killed his father and ate him. Doi is a psychoanalyst and discovered these patterns of patients through a one-on-one verbal therapy over a long period of time. IDAM, despite its providing a one-time and short drama, allows children to direct to the therapist their very *amae* toward their own mother. These dramas turn out to be a vivid representation of frustration toward their mother when dramas are seen from the viewpoint of transference of *amae* toward mother. Doi's patterns are useful to understanding children's performance in drama.

In addition, it is very compelling that two kinds of *amae* are presented:

> [A] primitive one which is sure of a willing recipient and convoluted one which is not sure if there is such a recipient. The former kind is childlike, innocent and restful: the latter is childish, willful and demanding: to put it simply, good and bad *amae*, so to speak. (2005, p. 141)

Thus, *amae* of the three children was the latter, under which characters were childish, willful, and demanding, and the dramas made the therapist uncomfortable.

Reason (4) Children's actual physical violence in their dramas

As mentioned earlier, the fourth reason is actual physical violence by the three children. They used it because they were unable to remain in dramatic reality that provides a world of pretense.

At that time, Sally Bailey advised me to tell children in advance that there is a rule that they must not actually hit someone or throw something during a drama. This is because it is difficult to draw a line between the two realities once it starts, as I have experienced. Until then, I had not told the children such a rule in advance as no problem like this had ever occurred. Actually, even in the scene in which they hit me, they had just pretended to do so.

Japanese clinical psychologist and play therapist Akuta (1999) notes that in a situation in which "a child cannot move forward without directing aggressive feelings at a therapist," when the restriction of such behavior can lead to "the risk of the complete denial of the whole existence of the child, it is possible to exceed the restrictions in the end" (p. 92). As an example, she cites a case where a play therapist performed a scene in which he was hit hard by a child client with a sword and then ground into mincemeat and "eaten" in every session and continued to endure severe pain. According to the therapist, he endured the pain, thinking that "it has its own significance that he was turned into mincemeat and that if he fell down there, the play would not work." Although Akuta shows "respect for the great tolerance of the therapist, who continued to endure heavy physical attacks," there should never be actual physical attacks in therapy settings at any time.

In addition, from the perspective of a client, overcoming the negative feelings through acts that actually hurt a therapist entails great danger. The experience of actually hitting the therapist hard while being driven by a real feeling of anger and seeing the victim enduring being hit without resistance could further promote such negative behavior and encourage violence.

In the case of dealing with children who are facing such serious circumstances or emotional problems that they cannot follow the rule of no actual hitting, it is an important job and responsibility of a therapist to provide an opportunity in which they can heal themselves by pretending to do so.

In Developmental Transformations, in order to establish playspace, three ethical conditions need to be present; "restraint against harm" ("defined boundaries between representation of aggression/sexuality and reality"), "discrepant communication" ("knowing this is pretend"), and "mutual agreement" (between client and therapist) (James et al., 2005, p. 73). According to Johnson (2000), "Play ends when harm occurs; play deteriorates rapidly when harm is possible" (p. 106). He notes that when the client's action or emotion such as anger get "too real" during the sessions, the therapist "articulate[s] a boundary condition" (p. 106) and that everything that happens in a play or drama space is pretend.

Furthermore, being able to *pretend* to make a physical attack shows that they have achieved double self-consciousness in which they can escape from the state of being controlled by an intense feeling of anger and keep a little distance from it while expressing it. Ensuring that they have a good understanding of the framework of a drama will also help to give them mental allowance.

Emotional violence and effect of Transference within Drama

We just reviewed the prohibition of actual physical attack in the previous section. Emotional violence, i.e., throwing negative feelings in words and attitudes, should also be mentioned here. The explanation by McMahon (2009) will help us understand how it affects a therapist. She describes the distress of a worker who conducts a play session in a home for abused children as follows:

> We may become afraid of our own angry and punitive feelings towards the child as we receive the full force of the child's anger in play sessions and have to resist the urge to retaliate. Or we may be so busy defending ourselves and the environment from the child's anger that we have no opportunity to create the mental space to reflect on and to respond to the child's communication. The victim has become a prosecutor. This can be alarming, and we may feel overwhelmed. . . . We feel useless and helpless, even contaminated. (p. 80)

Although interaction with children will be sometimes very challenging for the therapist as described above, their expression of negative feelings in words and attitudes must not be suppressed. Regarding what to do in such a case, McMahon (2009) proposes, "We need continually to remind ourselves that the attack is not personal but a re-enactment of the children's feelings towards parents whom they feel have let them down" (p. 80). This should be very helpful. However, in the case of therapy without the framework of a drama, it may be difficult to deal with the client's negative feelings expressed toward the therapist as they keep taking the role of a client and a therapist both inside and outside of the therapy, because therapy and ordinary reality are usually separated only by the *space* of the therapy room and the *time* of the therapy. The framework of drama can draw the line between therapy and ordinary reality most appropriately, making it possible to contain the feelings evoked by transference "dramatically," i.e., through fictional roles during special time on a special drama stage. I have named this process as *Transference within Drama*. Clients can transfer their feelings in the drama and then return to the original therapist-client relationship at once after the deroling process. Pendzik (2012) also refers to transference during drama therapy, citing the words of Jennings (1996), as follows, "dramatic reality offers a setting in which these concealed aspects can be brought safely into the light" (p. 206). Therefore, in the context of dramatic reality, the expression of negative feelings could be permitted and accepted. This structure of drama therapy is excellent, and it also deflects damage from the therapist. IDAM enables a therapist to conduct sessions comparatively free from the issue of transference due to the very short length of the dramas and very few times of the sessions, and the structure of the space with witnesses watching the dramas.

When I later implemented long-term drama therapy for abused children in an orphanage in Japan, I applied the lessons learned from the sessions in **I**'s class. Before each session, the children and I confirmed the promise that they must not actually attack someone and should just pretend, and they followed it. The children there always heavily rebelled, bullied or killed me in the role of a mother (Onoe, 2014), but these feelings directed at me were firmly confined in the dramas. During the snack time that was given after the session as a part of deroling process, they came to me with a childlike attitude for a comfortable time together.

Ending of drama and child's *Power to Heal Oneself*

Now, I will look back on the two dramas with **I** from four factors discussed above which hindered the flow of drama.

First, "four-part organization" of Japanese narratives manifested beautifully in these dramas. In addition, both **I** and I were able to end the drama in a good mood.

It was a great realization for me that he had the inner strength of heart to bring a happy ending. Being able to do this in a drama means that he has the power to do so in real life as well. This is the ability that everyone has. Accordingly, it may be said that children who cannot bring a happy ending nor enjoy a sense of unity with other have a heavier burden on their heart at the moment. A child's state of mind is portrayed in one drama as a microcosm of real life, although IDAM is only a few minutes long. I have, therefore, decided to call this the "power to heal oneself," the ability to bring a happy ending to an improvisational drama. In other words, *looking at the ending of a drama serves to assess the child's power to heal.*

Secondly, it turned out that **I** was able to enter dramatic reality, remain there, and enjoy the drama in that world, and come back to ordinary reality without a problem in both dramas. He had the ability to clearly distinguish between two realities. In particular, it was very impressive that after the second drama ended, he soon returned to his real self, a fifth grader, and expressed his thanks to me, although he let me feed him some steak like a spoiled little child in the drama a short time before. **I** must also have had more strength than the other three children concerning this ability as Bailey (2010) states, "Understanding the difference between real and non-real is crucial to identity formation and the ability to relate to others. Part of this is interwoven with the development of the self" (p. 28).

Thirdly, his rebellious emotion calmed down soon, and conflicts with the mother in both dramas were resolved in the scene. He does not fall into any of the three mental conflict situations of Doi, and he was able to *amaeru* on the mother. His *amae* was obviously a good one which is "childlike, innocent and restful." Stated differently, it is presumed that he had a sure image of "a willing recipient" (Doi, 2005, p. 141), whereas the other three children did not at that time.

Fourthly, he never used actual physical attack, nor prolonged emotional attack against the therapist.

These four factors are useful indicators to understand reasons of discomfort by the therapist in IDAM and to know if anything is hindering children from having the power to heal themselves and their situations.

As an objective fact, **I** was diagnosed with ADHD and was seeing a psychiatrist regularly and taking medication. Also, the information from the homeroom teacher acknowledged **J**, **K**, and **L** were "ordinary children" without particular problems. At least they never left the classroom during classes like **I** did.

It is both very interesting and enlightening that the evaluation of **J**, **K**, **L**, and **I** (as well as the diagnosis for **I**), which was made by observing their everyday life and surrounding context only from a superficial and phenomenal perspective, was reversed when their dramas were seen with a focus on the power to heal themselves. After reflecting on these dramas intensely, this has been a fascinating and significant discovery for me.

4 "RECONCILIATION" WITH THE THREE CHILDREN

Surprising "reconciliation"

While I was concerned about the fact that we were unable to bring an appropriate "ending" to the dramas with **J**, **K**, and **L**, "reconciliation" between us came around on the day of the third session! On that day, a closure to the three dramas was waiting for the three children and me, each in a wonderful and unexpected way.

After the session ended and all children had left the classroom, **J** rushed to me and said, "My real self is different from me in the drama I performed." He carried out deroling himself. I felt that he realized it after the session and that he needed to confirm this important fact then and there before I left the school. He understood the difference between dramatic reality and ordinary reality, and came to tell me that his real self did not have that anger towards me and that I was not the person that his real self should be fighting with! From the perspective of the 6-Key Model, it was the moment when "the ability of participants to respond to what they did while they were in dramatic reality" (Dickinson & Bailey, 2024, p. 140) was shown, which is the most important ability in the 5th Key "The Response to Dramatic Reality from the Outside." I said with a smile that I knew, because that was just a drama, and placed my hands on his shoulders affectionately. Listening to me, he ran out of the classroom with a smile of relief and satisfaction. We were both filled with joy. This event made me feel that we had reached a real reconciliation, completely different from the last time when I forced him to shake hands as a matter of form. I certainly felt that it brought peace to our hearts.

I continued to consider what he was trying to dig up in the garden persistently in the first part of the drama and what it symbolized. Later, I realized that he might have been trying to dig up his anger and rebellion, which were buried deep in the garden in his heart. The drama with him began with a scene in which he refused to go to school and "literally" threw the feelings dug out of him (which were embodied in the slippers and the ball) at me. According to Doi's three patterns of mental conflict caused by the lack of experience of *amae*, **J** falls into "People who find themselves without desire to *amaeru* and have a strong sense of distrust." However, when he came to me to make sure I understand "his real self," I was able to feel that there surely appeared to be trust between us and this trust could give him a foundation to express *amae* toward the mother figure later.

In the case of **K**, it was obvious that he had worked to actively participate in the third session, cherishing every moment and enjoying all activities to his heart's content, as he wrote in his first letter to me. When I offered a drink break because the children were sweating after playing the game "a scene from daily life," **K** came to me to ask whether I would continue the same game after the break. This was the only time that I had personally talked with him outside the drama. When I answered that I planned to do something else, he strongly begged me to allow him to introduce one more scene from his daily life. I was a little surprised that he asserted himself with a strong emotion although he was usually expressionless, and agreed to his request, considering that it must be very important and meaningful for him. Of three patterns of the mental conflict, **K** is considered to fall into "People who cannot *amaeru* even if they want to do so." His expression of a strong request to me like this shows his accomplishment of *amae*, which can be regarded as "good *amae*." It was, then, good for him that his *amae* was accepted by me.

After the drink break, **K** played a scene from his daily life in which he woke up in the morning in his room. When the alarm clock rang, he reached out to stop it sleepily and crawled out of bed to get up. He then said with great distaste, "Not again! Mom is still sleeping. Ah, I have to eat bread alone again!" The scene lasted only about 20 seconds. We all mirrored his behavior and words to share his feelings. **K** looked very happy. It was this scene that he really wanted to play and share with all his classmates and me! It was a precious 20 seconds. Recalling **K**'s performance in the drama of his repetitive complaint to the mother, saying she had thrown away his toys, and then of his "taking his own life in a car accident," I was led to vividly imagine **K**'s eating bread alone at home. Perhaps the situation of his mother in real life and his daily life was condensed into this scene.

After that, I conducted a Jizo drama. When I asked the children if anyone wanted to play an imaginary scene with me, as expected, **K** was the first to volunteer. He wanted me to play the role of Jizo and made a wish to me, saying, "Please make me peaceful forever from now on. In addition, may the world also be peaceful!"

Many children make wishes, such as "I want to be smart," "I want to get along with my friends," and "I want to be rich." However, hearing him wish for peace, I was deeply touched. **K**, who had, in reality, climbed on the railing of the outer corridor on the third floor, indeed did not have "peace" in his mind. Playing the role of Jizo, I answered, "All right. I'll protect you and the world forever." (This answer was of course given by Jizo in his imagination.) What was needed between him and me was not exactly "reconciliation." He may have used "violence" (bashed his forehead against mine) in the drama partly to conceal his embarrassment, and I thought that he had already "paid" for his "violence" by "killing himself" in the drama (although he paid too high a price). The very ending of the drama may have been his way of expressing "reconciliation" with the "mother" to whom, he might have thought, he could not properly respond and felt sorry. If he was not used to having his mother take care of him in real life, it is no wonder that he did not know how to respond to the care offered by me, as his mother in the drama. His "suicide" and his "rebirth" urged by the therapist can be interpreted as the convergence of feelings that he expressed in the drama and the reflection of the desire to repair his relationship with his mother. Later, he externalized sadness, which he felt when he ate breakfast alone, in the scene that *he wanted to play* and felt satisfied by having his sad feelings accepted by others. He then wished for peace for himself and the world, had Jizo grant his wish, and reached a happy ending. It was an inevitable process for him. It would be no exaggeration to say that his drama saved him from the shadow of death. It can also be inferred that he had a deep desire to escape from the shadow of death. It was Jizo who saved him, or more accurately, his own zest for life that created such a Jizo.

Regarding **L**, I saw him outside the classroom during a drink break. When I was walking around, he asked me what the matter was. I answered that I needed some water and asked where I could get some. He seemed happy to help me and hurriedly guided me to an automatic water fountain, saying, "The water over there is lukewarm and doesn't taste good. There is cold and delicious water here, so come over here!" After drinking some water, I said to him, "Wow, it's cold and tastes good. Thank you for telling me where I can drink delicious water." He seemed to be pleased to accommodate me and gave me a big smile. Completely different from the rebellious child in his drama, he then behaved childlike and innocent. Although there were many children in the corridor during the break, **L** and I met with perfect timing, when we were alone with each other. I have experienced the occurrence of coincidences many times when a deep psychotherapy process seems to be in progress. At the end of the drama in the previous session, **L** had continued to make unreasonable demands, ordering me to bring some water. At this time, however, he let me drink delicious water. It was such a miraculously symbolic event that we could not have expected a more perfect reconciliation and happy ending. Of three patterns of the mental conflict, **L** falls into "People who do not feel satisfied no matter how much they *amaeru*." He did *amaeru* very much by requesting various kinds of drink. Conversely, at the water fountain, he was not the person to *amaeru* on me, but was letting me drink cool and fresh water, and was happy to see me *amaeru* on him. This realization is quite suggestive and intriguing.

The Power to Heal Oneself and significance of repeating

The "reconciliation" with the three children completely healed my heart, and there is no doubt that it was the same for them. It may not be appropriate to express that "a therapist is healed by the therapy that they provided to a client." However, I have come to understand that the client can achieve true healing when both the therapist and the client feel good. This is a fairly important understanding through intersubjectivity. Especially in IDAM, whether or not a client has healed themself can be judged by whether or not the therapist who plays opposite them feels good, although it is of utmost importance that the therapist feels good not for themself but for the child. This is quite an easy-to-understand criterion.

On the day that I was to leave the school, the three children created a happy farewell scene. They brought about this "reconciliation with the therapist" for themselves. It is likely that this enabled them to acquire an ability to create healing together with other and take the first step in fostering the power to heal themselves. Takeuchi (1999) notes that "a healer" is a person who encourages and supports people to "heal themselves." The therapist's role in IDAM is to accept, empathize, contain, and support clients through improvisational dramas. Patricia Sternberg (1999) said in a class that a therapist acts as "a catalyst" that brings about healing to others. This is correct in a sense. However, the dictionary tells us that "a catalyst does not change itself." When a client heals (changes) themself, I also heal (change) myself. In that sense, a therapist is not a catalyst. I say that a therapist is a client's partner who aims to share a good space and time for both to heal themselves.

Carlson & Shield (1990) notes the following:

> The quality of the healing relationship rather than the technique may be the hidden foundation for healing. . . .It is this special bond, created from compassion, trust, and the willingness to move forward together, that transforms the process from curing to healing. . . .In the presence of this relationship, both healer and client explore the depth of their experiences and resources. It is through this unity that ***both parties*** can indeed be healed. (Underlined by the author.) (p. 85)

As I recall, on the day when I performed the dramas with the three boys, I experienced a sense of incompetence because the drama did not finish in some good way. Yet, I was able to learn that even if I felt that I could not do anything for a client, "something" might be potentially progressing toward the next step. In the first session, I told the class that the sessions would be conducted three times. The three children firmly recognized this at an unconscious level and perfectly brought about "reconciliation" with me in the third session as if they had planned it this way. I am sure that "something" was ripening deep in their hearts during the period between the second and third sessions. It was also great learning from an actual experience that it is important to tell clients in the first session how many sessions they would have. On conducting brief drama therapy, Gersie (1996) notes that: "The preordained time limit then encourages both drama therapist and client to focus on [their issues] and to use [the given methods] most likely to produce optimum development" (p. 9).

In addition, as an important finding about repetition, I have realized that it is necessary not only to repeat the same thing but also to *continue to express* the same feeling, which is an important step toward change, resolution, and healing. **J** continued to take a fighting pose against his mother indefinitely while holding clappers in both hands. **K** endlessly continued to say that his mother had thrown away his toys. **L** endlessly continued to order drinks. When I look back now, their repetition strikes me with amazing significance. I tried to accept their repetition as much as possible while mirroring their actions and feelings. The seeds of their changes, which occurred on the day of the third session, had already sprouted in these repetitions.

Why does repeating the same thing in a drama bring about a change? As the therapist mirrors the client's action and emotions, both of them *repeat* the same actions or *thoroughly* absorb the same emotions to the extent that both will reach some sort of saturation, which then will take the therapy to the next stage. This is one of the most therapeutic moments. When you are limited to just mirroring a client, displaying the same behavior, and empathizing with them, you are still in the early stage of therapy. A client, repeating a certain performance, may encounter such emotions as truly disgusting feelings or an earnest hope for an action, spirally yet clearly.

It is just like the way milk becomes solid as butter when it is stirred constantly. The feelings that have become clear and visible through these processes are highly recognizable. It is not until then that you can carefully foster these feelings or throw them away if they are not necessary. In this way, it becomes possible to bring about a transformation.

Pendzik's 5th Key (Response) concerns the processing and evaluation of the experience of dramatic reality upon return to ordinary reality. "It gives an indication of the person's ability to process and integrate subjective experiences" (Pendzik, 2012, p. 205). I interpret the reconciliation with the three children as the 5th Key for them. The following letters that I received after the sessions also show their ability to do so.

Letters from the three children

J's letter:

> Hello. Thank you very much for your drama therapy. I enjoyed the drama therapy very much. I want you to come again, if possible. At first, I was worried about what drama therapy was. But when I actually participated in your sessions, I found it was really fun. I thought I wanted to experience more. Since the sessions were conducted only three times, I felt sad in the third session, thinking this was the last one. But I enjoyed the last session to the fullest.

K's letter:

> Ms. Onoe, how are you? I'm fine. I love drama therapy sessions. I want to take the session every week. I have learned a lot in your sessions. Firstly, I have learned to imagine, and secondly, how fun it is to

perform a drama. . . .I felt like I spent a lot of time in your sessions although they were conducted only three times. I think that's because I've made so many memories. My most enjoyable memory is the Jizo drama I performed at the very end of the sessions. Onoe-sensei, thank you very much.

L's letter:

Hello. How are you? I'm really fine. Thank you very much for your sessions in this term. . . .I think drama therapy is fantastic. The reason is that drama therapy is so much fun. We laughed a lot, got impressed a lot and imagined a lot. What I found particularly interesting was the dramas in which a child was about to be late for school in the morning. I enjoyed the dramas very much. Please come again in the third term if possible. Goodbye until we meet again.

I have learned so much from the series of dramas with these four children, including **I**. Higashiyama (1982), a Japanese clinical psychologist, notes, "Therapists almost always face problems and feel depressed when they go beyond their current growth stage. Otherwise, they cannot move on to the next stage" (p. 212). I do not know whether or not I was able to grow. However, it is not an exaggeration to say that I felt like I went over the mountain at that time. If I had gone over the mountain, the children must have done so too. At least I earnestly hope so.

One of the things that they overcame is undoubtedly the image of a Terrible Mother (Neumann, 1974), which is a kind of archetype of a Great Mother. The monster that **I** drew on the blackboard is exactly a terrible mother. However, he soon found pleasure in his mother's words when she said that she would go to the hospital to have her split personality cured and in eating steak with her. This may possibly mean that his Terrible Mother is less formidable than expected. In contrast, I suspect that the fact that the dramas with **J**, **K**, and **L** came to a standstill may show that their Terrible Mothers are quite formidable. Nevertheless, the three children actually fought well! **J** literally continued to fight with his mother, who had "killed his father and friend and ate them," without easily forgiving her. **K** also continued to challenge his mother, who was not taking care of her child, saying that "you threw away my toys." **L** continued to battle with his mother by ordering drinks one after another without compromise.

Paradoxically, however, their fighting concurrently provided an opportunity to have an experience of *amae*. The fighting in the dramas can be interpreted as bad *amae*, and "reconciliation" and expressing their feelings in the letters outside the dramas as good *amae*. As Doi (1961, p. 200) states, "It is in the relationship with the actual therapist that patients experience the happiness of genuine *amae*." It may be considered that these boys condensed the psychotherapeutic process and lived their lives to the fullest.

The therapist may feel only discomfort while playing a drama with children and be unable to know why. This is what is explained in Pendzik's Key 6: The Meta-Reality—The Unmanifested Subtext. Exploring this unknown situation led to realization that children were then going under a meaningful process and a drama not going well has a profound significance for them. Expressing what children want to and have to let out was essential and critical for their well-being. They conveyed this fact to me through an amazing reconciliation between us finally. In addition, their dramas with no ending seem to show that they have resilience and that they have achieved further growth through the whole process of three IDAM sessions. Each of them comprised a great journey of a hero.

Children I encountered through IDAM

Many of the elementary school students with whom I have been involved so far have felt stressed and frustrated. They include:

- Children who want to rebel against their mothers/caregivers.
- Children who want to more *amaeru* on their mothers/caregivers.
- Children who are not praised or acknowledged by their mothers/caregivers and therefore have low self-esteem.
- Children who are tired of behaving like a good child (for instance, playing the role of the eldest son or daughter, etc.).

In addition to worries at home, they have other worries, including worries about their studies at school and their relationships with friends. Moreover, they may be under major stress just like adults while living amid the storms of an unstable modern society.

Children are not good at verbally expressing their mental state. If they are provided with the opportunity to express and objectify such stress in an appropriate way at an appropriate time, there is a high possibility that their problem can be quickly resolved even if something has already become an issue in their daily life. I expect that **IDAM** will play a key role in the future as one of the major approaches to realize this.

5 ADDITIONAL IMPRESSIONS BY MORE CHILDREN

"When I take part in a drama therapy session, I feel refreshed after it's over." E.T.

"After I finish playing in a drama therapy session, my stress is relieved." J.S.

"The drama therapy sessions remained in my heart. When I gave my performance in front of my classmates for the first time, I felt very shy. But when I expressed my feelings with the word 'Ah,' I felt refreshed. For me, it was a refreshing game that relieved my stress. When the third session came to end, I didn't want the session to end, and I felt I would be sad. Yet, my heart has been warm and pounding strongly until now. Thanks to drama therapy, I can now laugh more than before." Y.I.

"Although I forgot the name of the character, both the character and I were similar in terms of cowardice. Watching and performing the drama, I felt my spirit emerge." H.H.

"Although I had pain in my legs due to a disease, I forgot the pain when I was playing with my classmates in your session." K.D.

"I had such a pleasant and enjoyable experience that it would be difficult for me to write all of my impressions in a letter." N.T.

"I don't think I've ever had such a fun time before." A.D.

"I never thought drama therapy could be so much fun. I was late for the third session because I had a nosebleed. I was preoccupied with the fact that it was your last session. But I really enjoyed it." H.K.

"I felt very shy in the first session. But in the second and third sessions, shyness went far away." T.K.

"I now have a little bit more courage to do what I couldn't do before out of shyness. I feel like I could change myself thanks to your sessions. It's very sad that there were only three sessions. They were so much fun that I wanted to take your session three times a week." E.U.

"In a drama therapy session, I was able to give a performance in front of my classmates although I seldom raised my hand and spoke in other class lessons. I had the most fun performing dramas through ad lib." F.O.

"I didn't expect much from the session without knowing anything. But once the session started, it was so much fun that I didn't want it to end. In the end, while I didn't want a parting, all miscellaneous worries seemed to have gone away from me. I enjoyed your session very much. Since then, I've been doing my best to make everyone burst out laughing without worrying about my figure!" A.S.

"I was very stressed out about my family. However, after taking a drama therapy session, I've been able to have a lively life with no stress. . . .What has changed in me since I received the session is that now I can speak up in class. I was unable to speak in class until recently. But I can now speak in class without much difficulty in front of my classmates. Although I wonder how I have been able to do so. . . .it's all thanks to drama therapy." Y.K.

Extended Application of IDAM to Adults

Five

This chapter describes how IDAM can be applied beyond child therapy. When I first developed IDAM, I recognized that I had created a therapy approach for children. Later, through many of my classes and trainings of IDAM for graduate students and trainees, I came to realize the significance of using the same process for adult clients. In classes students are inevitably assigned to take a "role of a child." Their reactions toward the "mother" and drama processes often turn out to be similar to those which I encounter with "real children." I have been impressed that even a "healthy group" of adults let out various emotions harbored inside, receive healing from drama experience of being accepted by a "mother," and gain insightful self-awareness when facing a "mother" as they play a role of a "child." I thought that it would be clinically and theoretically much suited to apply IDAM to adult clients who were unable to receive sufficient care from their mother (caregiver) during childhood, and to have them experience to *amaeru* directly on the mother in a drama.

1. APPLICATION TO ADULT CLIENTS—WOMEN WITH ADDICTIONS

(Reprinted and updated from Onoe, A. (2024). The significance of mother-child improvisational drama in drama therapy for women with addictions: From the perspectives of attachment trauma and mentalizing. *Japanese Journal of Group Psychotherapy,* 40 (2), 220–227. *With permission from Japanese Association for Group Psychotherapy.*)

(1) Issues and purposes

For many years, I have practiced drama therapy at an addiction recovery facility for women in Japan, and have contributed to enhancing the motivation for recovery by improving interpersonal relationships in the community to which they belong, preventing relapse, reducing

DOI: 10.4324/9781003565062-6

anxiety, and providing crisis intervention (Onoe, 2013). Most of them are "adult children," many of whom have the experience of abuse and trauma related to attachment and *amae*. This makes it difficult for them to form and maintain close and stable human relationships (Allen, 2013; Flores et al., 2004). Flores (2004) identified addiction as an attachment disorder and asserts that it is important to provide care and treatment to addicts so that they can acquire the ability to maintain healthy attachment relationships with others. "Insecurity in attachment relationships is a signal of limitation in mentalizing skills" (Fonagy et al., 2002, p. 7). Many of the women in the facility do not seem to have received appropriate emotional mirroring from or were not given affect regulation functioning by their caregiver during childhood, and therefore they have difficulty in affect regulation and mentalizing. Irwin & Dwyer-Hall (2021) mention in a joint research between a drama therapist and a supervisor on Mentalization-Based Treatment for children and adolescents that "the core goal of drama therapy is to foster awareness and control of one's emotional life and interactions with others, i.e., affect regulation, a capacity closely related to mentalization" (p. 2).

(2) Features and structures of the sessions at this facility

The drama therapy in this facility is trauma-informed. This is when a therapist conducts drama therapy not directly focusing on trauma but knowing that the clients have had trauma experiences. Johnson and Sajnani (2014) state that "[m]ost drama therapists have utilized the *creative/expressive paradigm*, which asserts that allowing free expression of thoughts and feelings in an imaginative, creative context is a path toward well-being" (p. 14). The practice at this facility also intends to allow creative and free performance under a fictional setting.

IDAM for adults is equally safe and efficient as for children because it does not require disclosure of what actually happened or what the mother in real life did or said. Adults, however, need some careful procedure of creating trust in a group and attentive warm-up steps before playing a drama due to their difficulty to be immediately absorbed in drama as children and their tendency to mind being watched by an audience more. So, I devised a new kind of a mother (caregiver)—child drama in Part Two, though the structure of Three Parts remains the same.

(3) Intention of new drama (Drama 1 in Part Two)

Structure of a session Part One: Warm up games Part Two: Drama 1: Mother (Caregiver)-Child drama with all the clients acting simultaneously Drama 2: IDAM (one-on-one drama with a therapist) Part Three: Closure

In this drama (Drama 1), all participants pair off, playing simultaneously, and one plays the role of a mother (caregiver) and the other plays the role of a child in some given situations, switching roles, and experiencing both roles. Here, while playing the roles of an amusement park clerk, a zoo clerk, and a hostess at an inn, I guided the players so that they could perform a scene where the mother can take care of the child.

The uniqueness of this drama is that it has no audience as everyone plays in pairs at the same time, which diminishes tension of playing and allows freer acting for participants who are unfamiliar to performance. Group cohesion heightens as all feel the group's intention of creating the same scene together. Also, the scene of many people playing together produces the atmosphere of being in a real amusement park, for instance.

This setting served its purpose very well. This drama is to provide the opportunity for participants to regain the free spirit of children and experience the joy and peace of mind of being fully cared for by a trusted adult when they play the role of a child and, in turn, to elicit an "internal nurturing parent" (Emunah, 2020, p. 125) and to provide the opportunity to experience taking care of the "child," who in fact exists within them, when they play the role of a parent. Every time, I told the participants carefully this purpose and intention of this drama. While people need the experience of being cared for by others, they should also be able to take care of themselves with love. Therefore, participants are offered a chance to care for themselves by taking care of the "real child" in front of them, played by other participants, in which they can practice caring and nurturing themselves and which itself is a process of psychoeducation, even when they do not understand an ideological object such as an imaginary target in their head and the so-called "inner child."

In fact, several participants said, "In a self-help group, I heard that it was good to heal the inner child, and I understood what that meant for the first time through the concrete experience in this drama." The participating members were in diverse situations, including singles, people raising children, and those who had trouble raising children in the past, and the work also served as parent training in a broad sense.

After a drama of all participants playing together, I practiced IDAM in each session with me playing the role of a mother. I performed a drama, taking the exact same stance as when I do it for children and as if the participants were children.

(4) Presentation of sessions

The following section presents Part Two of three sessions.

1. Part Two of the first session

Drama 1: Riding Ferris wheel with mother (caregiver)

The scene has a sudden failure incident of the wheel stoppage, which is meant to provide a child with the experience of assurance by the mother. Clients later gave remarks about this incident similar to the following ones: "It instinctively made me look into the face of the adult nearby. I did not trust an adult, but this emergency let me utter to her, 'I am scared' for the first time" (Remark 1). "I could not say 'I'm scared' when I was a kid. This time, though, I could tell her, 'I am scared to ride this, no, I don't wanna do it,' with *amae* to her, and felt like being protected" (Remark 2). **M** (alcoholic, diagnosed as borderline personality disorder (BPD)) referred to her discovery from playing a role of mother as follows: "The child played by my partner besought me, 'Stay with me, I need nothing else,' and then, I clearly had a sudden insight on my self-satisfaction of merely buying my own child things only" (Remark 3).

Drama 2 (IDAM): A scene of home when a child goes to school in the morning

At first participants had a bit of tension playing a drama, but the therapist's acceptance and mirroring prompted more and more people to actively develop new stories. In one drama, the child asks the mother, "I don't wanna go to school, but I'll try, so walk with me to the school gate." In other dramas, the child decides to be absent and enjoys paintings with the mother, or the mother, also taking a day off and saying, "Let's skip our duties!" goes to an amusement park with the child. These dramas developed in a pleasant way.

"It was the first time in my life that I was able to have my mother all to myself. I was very happy that this came true, and I almost cried" (Remark 4). "I was healed by the words from the therapist who played the role of a mother because I had wanted my mother to say such words in the past" (Remark 5). Although the participants performed just a short drama lasting only a few minutes, many of them made these remarks. The group consisted of women in their 20s to 60s, but no matter how old they are, it is never too late to have this kind of experience. One of those who did not step forward to play a drama concurred, "Seeing others' dramas convinced me that I too wanted to '*amaeru*' on my mother like that. I wanted her to approach me like that" (Remark 6).

M did not play in Drama 2 (IDAM). She appealed, saying, "I felt envious of people engaging in *amae*. I can never *amaeru*. It's mortifying not to know how to *amaeru* on mother" (Remark 7). She made the same comment every time after IDAM dramas and sometimes excused herself from the room.

2. Part Two of the second session

Drama 1: A drama at a zoo

N (alcoholic, diagnosed with possible developmental disorder) reported that "I was often left alone (by my real mother when we went out). (In the drama) I confirmed many times with mom 'not to go anywhere' when I used a restroom, and I was much relieved to find out she did really wait for me" (Remark 8). In the latter half of the drama, I made a scene where I became an elephant and escaped from the cage, and **N** did not get scared but followed the elephant and enjoyed it. Then others copied her action and the drama became an event of laughing children following the elephant.

Drama 2 (IDAM): A drama where the mother brings sweets to the child's room after school

In one story, the child whined to the "mother" to do homework together and felt satisfied by being given her favorite sweets. Inspired by the previous drama, following dramas developed the contents of homework quite interestingly, which elicited much laughter. The last player quite seriously expressed an ambivalent feeling of "I don't want to go to school, but I don't want to run away from doing so." While mirroring her feelings and postures, I stayed spiritually as close as ever to her, and we figured out a solution together. Although she told me that she had been very hurt by a recent event, she commented, "The drama healed my heart and made me realize that I was under the delusion that I was hurt, which was my habit."

3. Part Two of the third session

Drama 1: A drama of a hot spring journey

As sessions progressed, it was evident that children came to behave more freely and mothers were willed to give children more enjoyment.

Particularly, "all members' dinner party" at an inn produced much excitement and was full of energy with the sound of laughter and the voices of participants who acted like spoiled and willful children. It was strongly felt that each participant was having a fulfilling time. The whole room was filled with a warm and happy atmosphere. We felt as if we were at a real party in an inn, with no alcohol, of course. I functioned busily as a therapist playing the role of the Okami, or the hostess at the inn, literally running all over the inn to realize everyone's dream, serving all guests and taking their photos as they ask for remembrance.

N commented that she discovered a true message from her own daughter. "When I was told by the person who played the role of my child, 'I felt lonely. I wanted you to focus only on me,' I cried because I felt like my own daughter had told me that. I myself used to take my daughter with me when I went out with my boyfriend. When I was told this in the drama, I realized that my daughter hated it, and I felt a strong sense of guilt" (Remark 9). As many as three more participants said to the extent that "Until now, I had thought that my parents didn't love me and didn't do anything for me. But this is not true. I remembered that they did various things for me" (Remark 10). For example, one of them said, "My real mother once shook off my hand when I tried to hold her hand. But, when I got ointment put on me by mom in the drama, I remembered that my real mother held my hand with her little finger. I wonder if she tried in her own way to connect with me despite her dislike of physical touch. I remembered that she baked me cookies when I avoided school attendance" (Remark 11). On that day, **M** remarked as follows most positively than ever before. "Although I would be unable to undo the past, I'm glad I played the role of a child. I was able to *amaeru* to the full without wishing that the mother (in real life) had behaved like this" (Remark 12).

Drama 2 (IDAM): <u>In the child's room, the same setting as in the second session</u>

Everyone laughed heartily at the scene where the child played the funny man and the mother the straight man, cooking together in the end. Moreover, as an effect unique to group therapy, the fun of creating a drama with everyone on the spot produced even greater effects. In the scene where the mother and the child went walking at the sea, all of the audience members spontaneously participated in the scene as surfers waving at them on the beach. This acting by everyone gave all participants a strong sense of contribution to building the scene together. All dramas had rich stories and developed to realize their wish and hope, most freely than ever. Lastly, **O** (with an eating disorder and diagnosed with ADHD) played a serious drama by acting the child who narrated to the mother about her trying situations in childhood. She refused to take sweets from the mother and continued to complain for eight minutes about her painful feelings of many years. "I have no place where I belong at school or at home. You are only interested in work and men . . . I'm devastated. I have no one to talk to, either. I miss you so much. I have a hard time going to school. It feels so unbearable right now. It's all your fault." The "mother," who was approached with languishing and straight eyes, sensed **O**'s dissatisfaction if given an immediate apology, so the mother carefully listened to her, thanked her for communicating her feelings, and finally apologized for her own actions, and continued to tell her that she did not have to go to school, while mirroring the same kind of serious emotions and facial expressions as hers. After this talking, the mother, intending to change her own affect to positive, said, "I would be happy if we can eat the sweets together soon." Then **O** smiled for the first time and held out her hands suddenly and said, "Due to my overeating, there are many hangnails on my fingers. I was told that I was malnourished." I was surprised to see that her hands were actually very rough. When I delicately wrapped her hands in my hands and gently stroked them with love, I felt her feelings relaxed. She smiled slightly in hesitation. She finally stopped blaming the mother and convinced herself, saying that she felt a little relieved. After the drama, she said, "I'm glad that I was able to verbalize my feelings. As you told me that I could be absent from school, I feel relieved. Thank you very much" (Remark 13).

(5) Discussion

Clients' remarks suggested that a change in cognition had occurred for them. This change was recognizable because the clients were adults with self-introspection and verbalization capabilities. The process of connecting their childhood and the present and various mentalizing processes occurred there. I will examine and reflect on the two findings mainly based on the clients' remarks.

1. Acquisition of satisfaction

The participants expressed that they were able to realize what they could not do in childhood and acquired satisfaction (Remarks 1, 2, 4, 5, 8, 12, 13).

Playing a role in a drama gives the performer a very "real" experience of emotion and body from the perspectives of time and space despite its format being fictional. This is known to be one of the very authentic effects of drama therapy. What is important here is that different from receiving empathy from the other by being told, "You had a hard time, didn't you?" in the talk "about her past," she actually materializes her desire "here and now" by having the "mother" accept her, apologize to her, and do something together with her. Jones (1996) points this out by quoting Wilder (cited in Langer, 1953, p. 307) who says that "theatre action 'takes place in a perpetual present time . . . On the stage it is always now'" (p. 47).

Although their childhood situation can be assumed as their persevering with isolation and helplessness (Remarks 1, 2), many seemed to have experienced a secure base in a drama. For instance, it is interesting to note that **N** (Remark 8) took the active and creative action of following the elephant. Her action was possibly induced by her experience of the secure base created through readjustment of her emotions by the "mother who waited for her outside the rest room." Kimura et al. (2020) also report that affect regulation in a therapy leads children to engage in unexpected plays or dialogues subjectively and creatively.

In Drama 2 (IDAM) as well, when the mother (the therapist) returns more secure emotions after mirroring emotions of the person's in a child role, many of them, one after another, started developing new stories actively and creatively by themselves. This phenomenon is the same as the one which appears when conducting IDAM with real children. **O** first experienced readjustment of emotions (i.e., the therapist mirrored her serious emotions, and returned her more positive emotions), then she initiated a new action (i.e., she held out her hands), which led to her to discover she felt relieved, possibly because she gained a sense of satisfaction and security. Since she is presumed to have had deep-rooted resentment, the drama seems to have had great significance for her as one big experience to deal with such emotion.

Some clients, who said that they were unable to *amaeru* because they did not know how to do it, were already able to do so next time by using a drama in which other clients *amaeru* as a model. There were other clients who were able to recognize the feelings of themselves and their parents for the first time by only watching others performing a drama, or some who said that they healed themselves just by witnessing a drama without performing it. Just like in the sessions with children, one of the reasons above could be said that the collective mind of the group broadens their experiences. Shteynberg and Apfelbaum (2013) emphasize the power of shared experience and watching together with others facilitates social learning, which also explains how the clients here were able to learn how to *amaeru* played and modeled by other group members. Shteynberg et al. (2020) say that people can achieve something more by collective learning, which cannot be gained individually.

As **M** (Remark 7) implies, it is easily understandable that some people have difficulty attending Drama 2 (IDAM), where one faces the parent properly. Even **M**, however, acquired in Drama 1 a clear, sudden insight into relations with the child (Remark 3) and a full experience of *amaeru* (Remark 12). It may be because Drama 1 has a higher level of fictionality and security as everyone plays together with less attention on each player. Remark 12 shows that she was able to live only here and now, rather than acting while being pulled by the past. In short, the structure of combining Drama 1 and Drama 2 (IDAM) worked successfully.

It was quite impressive that those who seemed to not have received care like this from their real parents provided the child with a very good care, especially in Drama 1. The benign side of their archetypal "mother" might have been awakened as they understood the purpose of the drama and are given a setting and space to be in a role of a mother. Some remarked that "In a role of a mother, I acted to realize the being that will be gentle and stand close to the child, which is missing in me." Participants proffered each other satisfaction of being cared for, drawing out their own potentiality.

2. Understanding multilayered affect

It is speculated that the participants existed at the same time as the person whose role they were playing and as the self who was playing the role.

Expressing with imagination the affect and situations of the role they are playing and of the role opposite themselves, participants seemed to achieve a multilayered understanding of the affect of the current self and of the past childhood, the affect of the parent when they were a child, and, for some participants, the affect of the real child of their own. There, the self who experiences oneself subjectively as the one playing the role and the objective self who is playing out there exist simultaneously, which enabled them to understand their several selves and others from multiple perspectives.

For example, there occur inner dialogues between the parent and the child in their roles and between the real parent and oneself for the audience, respectively. Furthermore, an inner dialogue may also appear between the actor themself and the audience. Remark 6 reveals that some could identify the affect of themselves and their parents for the first time by watching others perform a drama. Remarks such as 10 and 11 show that cognition of the real parents in the past changed in three clients.

It is possible that satisfaction and the sense of security affected one's way of looking at the past and brought about a positive perspective. Another issue is that people who had a trying time with their parents (who may have deficits in mentalizing) in their childhood behave in a way whereby they do not understand the feelings of their own children. This is called intergenerational transmission of non-mentalizing (Allen et al., 2008). However, Remarks 3 and 9, for instance, show the possibility that awareness through a drama will lead to new ways for performers to deal with their own children.

Understanding of emotions in the way described above may have helped them develop the mentalizing ability. During the time of sharing, participants as a whole appeared to be serenely in access with the past memory.

Having experienced the secure base in the drama, they were literally sharing with all others through careful verbalization of episodes of their original families and their own reminiscences with peer members and the therapist with whom they just exchanged their own experiences as a drama. It seems that they were able to reflect on happenings and the whole work with their feet grounded firmly because of multilayered formation of the secure base in the facility, in the drama group, and in the drama itself, which provided them with more kinship and capacity to share emotions with peers.

Okada, a Japanese psychiatrist who has treated many patients with attachment disorder, states (2011) that resuscitating a child's mind is key to recovery as well as doing to others what one wants one's parent(s) to do. These two processes are exactly what are realized in the two dramas of Part Two. Three of his treatment achievements attract my attention:

1. Patients have a period when they insist on selfish matters as if having regressed to be a child and troubling their parents. Clinician's full acceptance of this period gradually leads to recovery of stability (p. 268).

2. Patients gain perspective as a whole that their real parents tried to do what they could in their own way and provided them with love rather than the client getting stuck with a complete negation that everything was bad (p. 280).
3. Cases were quite successful when a patient took the role of one's own parent and tried to live in consultation with the inner parent existing in oneself.

These achievements resulted from treatment processes of long-term, individual verbal sessions. IDAM suggested a possibility that the same types of cognition changes and insights are achieved for more clients in a shorter period of time through dramatic reality created by IDAM for a group setting. While it may be hard to say if the same level of transformation occurs through only the three sessions as the one achieved above by Okada's patients, but at least, IDAM practices show that clients gain new insights with less pain for clients and less burden on therapists due to more acceptability of direct negative Transference within Drama than in reality.

(6) Conclusion

The main feature and significance of mentalizing lies in understanding the existence of both the self and others at the same time. It has the potential to be extended to the understanding that transcends the time.

Multilayered mentalizing occurred in these sessions through drama experience that encompassed time and space as they played on a number of dramas in a group, acting the roles of the child and the parent with peer members, with the therapist and also watching others play.

In addition, these dramas surely created an illuminating sense and new experiences different from the past ones within participants. Every one of them, though on a different level for each, must have felt communication and confidence with the archetypal "Mother" which exists in all of us. Although nearly half of the participants were already parents, many of them experienced a secure base possibly for the first time. They had never had such a "hands-on" opportunity to become a child and receive care from a mother and were not likely to have it again in the future.

It has been shown above that the very experiences like these are the specific feature of IDAM and can be part of the motivating power to understand the self and others, enhance personality and bring about changes. Throughout the dramas, the author felt as if real children were there playing. To sum up, those with attachment or *amae* trauma fictionally regressed into a child, experienced a new *amae* behavior in a drama, acquired mentalizing ability, and expanded it from fictional to real representation. This is the essence of the IDAM practice for adults.

The section concludes with the suggestion that IDAM does not target only children but is promising for a wider variety of populations. It would be great if readers could try it out on various populations and report what process should occur.

2. APPLICATION TO THE TRAINING OF (DRAMA) THERAPISTS

This training serves not only for a participant to be able to practice IDAM, but as a way to learn the essence of how to effectively reach out to people needing support and how to respect and accept the other's will and, at the same time, lead them forward. It is also useful as a way to allow a participant to realize their natural inclination and how they have human relationships/support relationships and gain an objective perspective of themself. Therefore, this training serves well even if trainees do not plan to use IDAM in the future, even if they do not plan to offer therapy for children, or even if trainees are clinical psychologists, therapists, or therapists in the making who do not plan to do drama therapy.

As a general flow, the training will proceed in the order of body mirror, voice mirror, and a mother-child drama.

(1) Body mirror

As the first work, participants do physical mirroring in pairs.

- *In reference to Emunah's Partner Mirror (2020, pp. 170–171), the pair face each other and make eye contact. One person moves slowly as a human, and the other acts as a mirror image in front of the person and imitates the partner.*
- *Once they get used to it, the person playing the role of a human changes facial expressions, and the person playing the role of a mirror image mirrors the partner's feelings as well.*
- *They reverse their roles at the second stage.*
- *At the third stage, the trainer instructs them to start mirroring without deciding who will play the role of a human (i.e., the leader) and who will play the role of a mirror image (i.e., the follower) and to naturally reverse their roles several times without using words during the stage.*

When the relationship between two people is viewed in real life, it would be unhealthy if one of them is always the leader or always the follower. Therefore, it is ideal to create a relationship where the leader and the follower naturally switch roles with each other. The intention of the work is to let the two feel such a relationship symbolically and concretely. When they become accustomed to mirroring each other at the first two stages, most of the pairs say that they felt most comfortable at the third stage. If things go well, they can spend time interacting with each other in a situation where they do not know which one is now playing which role. In other words, they can obtain a sense of unity, creating something together at the same time without using words. This is a profound work. Using this work as a metaphor for reality, participants can realize their natural inclination and how they have human relationships. It is recommended that they deeply reflect on what they have realized while connecting it with their own way of being and their support style.

This work is the first basic practice of IDAM.

(2) Voice mirror

- Participants pair off with a different person and mirror the partner by voice. One person makes a repeating sound with a rhythm (any sound such as ah ah . . .) so that the partner can easily mirror the other (to achieve the original purpose such as creating empathy and unity).
- The person playing the role of a mirror predicts what kind of voice will be uttered by the person playing the role of a human and lets out own voices at the same time while trying as much as possible to avoid deviation. Since it is easier to transfer feelings into the voice than in the case of body mirror, the person playing the role of a human utters voices with emotion, and the person playing the role of a mirror mirrors it. Only the mirroring tools have changed, and the essence of what is happening is the same as in the case of body mirror.

  The body also often moves spontaneously, which it may be difficult to avoid, but the main mirroring media should be through voice.
- They reverse their roles.
- At the third stage, as is the case for body mirror, they start mirroring without deciding which one plays which role.

When participants concentrate on the mirror work for a few minutes, they immediately know the partner's typical attitude. For instance, they understand whether the partner accepts the other, whether the partner withdraws into themself, whether the partner follows the other obediently . . . and that is, whether the partner has the will to interact in this relationship. If they have the power to introspect, they will realize that this simple work serves as an analogy for their own patterns and how they behave in human relationships. They can also know deeply about themself. Very symbolic and specific voices reveal the essence of the human relationship. This work does not require interactions by words that occur in normal life but uses only voice as the medium for interactions. How much they can realize interactions work as training and condense the interactions between the two. If you have time, practice with different partners a number of times, then, you will notice interactions each particular to a partner and learn more deeply.

(3) Mirroring between a therapist and a client through voice only

- Next, using the same *Voice mirror*, one person plays the role of a therapist and the other as a client.

The therapist is not expected to just lead or follow the client. This is common in other modalities of therapy. Initially, the therapist mirrors (follows) the client's current state. Then, the therapist creates a therapeutic process together with the client while naturally switching their roles. The therapist eventually needs to lead the client. In order to be able to do so, the first priority and most important thing is to thoroughly mirror the client and make the rhythms, voices, and feelings of the two in sync. If the therapist cannot do so, the existence of the two becomes completely inconsistent, inevitably making it impossible for the therapist to lead the client to a state of stability. Only after achieving synchronization can the therapist lead the client to transformation. The idea for this work was inspired by an episode in which Emunah calmed down a client who had been frightened in her dream after mirroring the movement and voice of the client and completely achieving synchronization.

- *First, the person playing the role of a client lets out their voice with the feeling of depression (Ah, ah . . . etc.), and the therapist follows (mirrors) it and synchronizes their voices, rhythm, and feelings.*

Even if the therapist can achieve synchronization, they will only be depressed together if the two just stay in sync. If it continues, the two may fall into further depression (as is often the case in real life).

- *After synchronizing with the client's depression, at some point, trying not to break the good flow, the therapist covertly changes from a mirror (follower) to a human (leader), and leads the client to raise their mood within the level in which they does not feel uncomfortable. (It is necessary to figure out good ways to do this, including increasing the pitch and speeding up the rhythm of the voices or using a different sound.)*
- *The person playing the role of a client must look the therapist in the eye.*

This whole activity is a training; it is not used for real clients. Therefore, it is considered that trainees generally have no difficulty making eye contact. However, in case a trainee has a tendency toward autism and feels it is difficult to look the other in the eye, it's good to have them practice building eye contact with playful games (Dickinson & Bailey, 2024, p. 306) preceding this training. Or, they can try the whole process of mirroring without making eye contact though it is less easy for a person in the role of the therapist to lead the client effectively enough to raise the client's mood.

The act of making eye contact is a statement that "I trust this therapist, and with the therapist's help, I am proactive in being involved in therapy." Basically, therapy is conducted based on such consent. If you do not make eye contact, this may serve as a symbol of not wanting to lift up your mood or follow this therapist.

When a client needs the help of someone else, they should have the ability to entrust themself to others, which will be part of their potential powers to save themself. If the client cannot do so, it is the therapist's job to first lead them to be able to entrust themself to the therapist. In this training, all this should be done with meaningless sounds only.

When the work ends, the person who played the role of a client conveys their frank opinions, such as "I felt like you were very considerate of me," "I felt better," and "You seemed to utter your voice on a different emotional level than mine." If possible, the "client" specifically tells the "therapist" that they felt that way because a meaningless sound emitted by the "therapist" at that time seemed to arouse such a feeling. Although there was a trainee who wanted to communicate with ordinary words (such as encouraging words), the significance of this work lies in not using words. It is an important practice to understand the essence of the other person and lead them through means other than words. Such interactions with sound only are rare in everyday life; however, if this work goes well, it will be understood that the "client" can be healed just by repeatedly letting out their voice together with the "therapist."

When I did this work in a pair with a graduate student, she actually told me that she was now healed. Although I did not know anything about her specific problems, I felt her painful emotions in her voice and realized that I was able to encourage her just with the sound of "ah ah." While words are very important, being able to heal or encourage a client without words is good training not only for creative arts therapists but also for talk therapists.

- *Next, the pair reverses their roles and practice a situation in which the person playing the role of a therapist calms down the person playing the role of an angry client.*

They experience a process in which the person playing the role of a therapist synchronizes with the feelings of the person playing the role of a client to understand the client's anger, and they calm down together. Although the therapist basically should not express feelings that are at a more intense level than those expressed by the client, there are exceptions. For instance, when the therapist feels that the client is withholding and expressing their anger at a modest level or feels that the client has not yet fully released their energy, it is recommended that the therapist expresses a slightly more intense level of anger by voice for a short time to communicate, "It is all right to express your anger a little stronger," and makes the client synchronize with the therapist.

When I actually did this in work with a graduate student, who played the role of an angry client, he admitted that he had been hesitant to express anger, but when hearing my voice, he had thought, "It is okay to express anger that much." My approach was to let him safely express anger by voice together with me to gradually lower the level of anger, and he said that this approach enabled him to command a bird's-eye view of his state of mind. Just at that time, I felt that "I acted only as a guide, and he calmed down his anger with his own power." When I mentioned this to him, he said that he felt the same way, and it turned out that what both of us felt was the same. This shows that just letting out your voice together for only a few minutes can become a very significant process.

When the work goes well between the pair, the person who plays the role of an angry client says that they felt soothed by voice alone and felt comfortable. Although this is certainly done by voice only, it is a work that an actual human being accomplished through mirroring. Since the partner is a human being, they cannot perform mirroring 100% the same way, which causes a slight difference in the way feelings are expressed. Such deviation can cause changes little by little. If mirroring is done 100% the same way, this cannot bring about changes. Needless to say, facial expressions, the mood from the whole body, and body movement as well as the voice are important. This is because the therapist gives consideration to the client with every ounce of their being.

(4) Mother-child drama in IDAM

When the practices described above are fully done, it is finally time to practice a mother-child drama in which trainees play the role of a child and a therapist, respectively. The essence of the work is the same as the above practices. However, trainees say that this is obviously the most difficult because they have to say their lines and proceed with a drama.

What is common for beginners is to carry on a conversation in an unchanging tone all the time. For instance, when the child is depressed and says, "I don't want to go to school," the therapist replies in the same mood, "What's wrong? Did something happen at school? Are you sick?" When the child answers, "I have a stomach ache," the mother says, "How does it hurt?" If a mother in real life responds in good faith like this, she is not doing anything wrong. In IDAM, however, there is no point in re-enacting a scene similar to real life. Such a scene is also not fun at all. This leads to a pattern in which the therapist and the child are in a state of being stuck and keep falling into depression together. Here, the therapist should gradually lead the child in order to move the drama forward, as in the previous voice practices. Another problem for beginners is that they tend to concentrate only on conversation as if in a counseling room. They need to remember to use body movements.

I have so far discussed how the setting of a mother-child drama instantly and effectively arouses the feelings of children and adult clients, and this also happens in the training. Furthermore, it has the potential to elicit trainees' own mother-child relationship and values. No matter how much trainees understand it in their head, beginners often become "just an ordinary mother." Therefore, I always have to say, "You are not a mother but a therapist who plays the role of a mother."

In verbal therapy, for instance, it is possible for a therapist to show "empathy and acceptance" by saying, "I can understand your feelings of not wanting to go to school," (even when the therapist's inner mind is posited differently). However, I do not know how many times I have seen dramas where as soon as a trainee takes on the "role of a mother," they instantaneously issue orders to go to school to a child wanting to skip school, and they never deviate from this stance without any playfulness. As an extreme example, there was a trainee to whom I said, "This is training, so just try and accept what the child is saying and tell them that they does not have to go to school as they wishes, not as you think they ought to," but who replied she could never say that. It feels like trainees are caught in their own mother's behavior or dominated by the strong norm that a child goes to school, constructed by society. This is a practice that frees them from such norms. The important points for the therapist are eliminating these biases, existing only for the best of the child present here and now while mentally and physically being in a not-knowing stance, and containing their whole self. This is what this training is all about.

When you play the role of the child, you can act freely as a child and your "inner child" comes out. This enables you to reflect on whether you felt satisfied in your childhood. Such reflection is important as a therapist as well. Moreover, the person who plays the role of a child always offers feedback to the partner who plays the role of a mother. As the child-therapist communicates the awareness that they gained by receiving mirroring and what made them feel good or bad, both can learn from each other. This is why psychotherapists in any modalities and for any populations learn from this training.

There is no single correct answer as to the best way to mirror or how the plot of a drama should develop. There are many possibilities. I want you to aim to create a meaningful place with a child while demonstrating a great deal of creativity, even in a short time drama.

Epilogue

In this book, I have discussed the importance of acceptance and mirroring, and of repeating these steps carefully and patiently. In nature, a tree standing in the snow waits for the time to sprout. In the blazing heat of midsummer, autumn lurks in wait. I realize the impermanence of nature. In exactly the same way, human feelings and relationships are always in motion. The children who appear in this book have taught me that the seeds of change are inherent in the repetition of the same thing that at first glance appears to be unchanged.

In life as well, there are times when we feel as if our suffering will last forever in the midst of its repetition, in particular, when we have bitter feelings and are involved in painful human relationships. However, in the suffering itself, there is hope for change. If we stop the action of repetition, the changes that are to be created may also stop at the same time. It is no exaggeration to say that repetition is necessary for change.

It is essential for us to perform a drama with undivided concentration and every ounce of our being. Children always go all out against the therapist in a drama. How wonderful it would be if we could make children, who have just begun their lives, let out and sublimate their worries, stress, and fears that they keep to themselves, while having fun together. What is stated here applies to adult clients who used to be "children" themselves.

Lastly, I will quote from a podcast of Jung and reiterate the features of IDAM. In Episode 210 *"Causal or Creative: Is History Destiny?"* of "This Jungian Life" (4/21/2022), the three Jungian scholars and practitioners—D. Stewart, L. Marchiano, and J. Lee—discuss a theme of causal or creative from a viewpoint of analytical psychology. They acknowledge as an important achievement of psychoanalysis the analysis of the effects of the past and outside situations upon individuals and the exploration into solutions of such effects. Yet, they argue that too much containment into such conditions may suppress the possibility for change. They continue that the key here is to internalize as the power within such energies from outside, and, to use it as a propellant force into the future. Likewise, one significant feature of IDAM is not only its exploration into the issues of the present or the past but also its offering chances of possible perspective for change from now. There, one is not caught up in the present or the past in a causal manner but can look to the future as one takes the causal in as part of the self. Children will see that the present is not absolute, and adults will realize that the past does not control, through a drama where they actually act out what they wish. The three Jungians explain the gist of the famous words by Jung (1968) as follows: A wise man does not seek causes of his sins in the past or in others but looks into his own heart sincerely and finds a new way.

Those who participate in IDAM at once shed their skins of "children" contained in the current situations, create a drama of their being its protagonist, and remove the hoop installed by the environment. Here, force is born to rid the causal and orient to the future. It will be my delight more than ever if IDAM could heal and liberate children and adults alike.

References

AC Japan. (2024). [In Japanese] https://www.ad-c.or.jp/campaign/nhk/nhk01.html

Akuta, N. (1999). *Yugiho [Play therapy]*. Shinyosha. [In Japanese]

Allen, J. G. (2013). *Restoring mentalizing in attachment relationships:Treating trauma with plain old therapy*. American Psychiatric Publishing.

Allen, J. G., Fonagy, P., & Bateman, A. W. (2008). *Mentalizing in clinical practice*. American Psychiatric Publishing.

American Psychiatric Association. (2013). *Diagnostic and statistical manual of mental disorders* (5th edition). American Psychiatric Publishing.

Aycox, F. (1985). *Games we should play in school*. Front Row Experience.

Badinter, E. (1982). *Myth of motherhood: An historical view of the maternal instinct*. Translated by R. De Garis. Souvenir Press Ltd.

Bailey, S. (2010). *Barrier-free theatre: Including everyone in theatre arts—in schools, recreation, and arts programs—Regardless of (dis)ability*. Idyll Arbor.

Balint, M. (1965). *Primary love and psycho-analytic technique*. Liveright Publishing Corporation.

Balint, M. (1968). *The basic fault:Therapeutic aspects of regression*. Tavistock.

Bandura, A. (1997). *Self-efficacy:The exercise of control*. W. H. Freeman.

Bateson, G. (1972). *Steps to ecology of mind*. Ballantine Book.

Bion, W. R. (1959). *Experiences in groups*. Tavistock.

Bouzoukiz, C. (2001). *Pediatric dramatherapy:They couldn't run so they learned to fly*. Jessica Kingsley.

Bowlby, J. (1969). *Attachment and loss, Vol.1. Attachment*. Hogarth Press and the Institute of Psycho-Analysis.

Brown, S., Cockett, P., & Yuan, Y. (2019). The neuroscience of Romeo and Juliet: An fMRI study of acting. *Royal Society Open Science*, 6: 181908. http://dx.doi.org/10.1098/rsos.181908

Carlson, R., & Shield, B. (1990). *Healers on healing*. Rider.

Causal or Creative: Is History Destiny? This Jungian life Podcast. (2022). https://podcasts.apple.com/nl/podcast/causal-or-creative-is-history-destiny/id1376929139?i=1000558221318

Dickinson, P., & Bailey, S. (2024). *The drama therapy decision tree: Connecting drama therapy interventions to treatment* (2nd edition). Intellect.

Doi, T. (1961). *Seishinryoho to seishinbunseki [Psychotherapy and psychoanalysis]*. Kanekoshobo. [In Japanese]

Doi, T. (1971, 2007, 2014). *Amae no kozo [Anatomy of dependence]*. Kobundo. [In Japanese]

Doi, T. (1981). *The anatomy of dependence*. Translated by John Bester. Kodansha International.

Doi, T. (1997). *"Amae" riron to seishinbunsekiryouho [Theory of "dependence" and psychoanalytical treatment]*. Kongoshuppan. [In Japanese]

Doi, T. (2005). *Understanding amae:The Japanese concept of need-love*. Global Oriental Ltd.

Doi, T. (2009). *Rinshoseishinigaku no hoho [Methodology for clinical psychiatry]*. Iwasakigakujutu shuppannsha. [In Japanese]

Donath, O. (2017). *Regretting motherhood*. North Atlantic Books.

Erikson, E. (1940). Studies in the interpretation of play: Clinical observation of play disruption in young children. *Genetic Psychology Monographs, 22*, 557–671.

Emunah, R. (2020). *Acting for real: Drama therapy-process, technique and performance* (2nd edition). Routledge.

Endo, T. (2012). Atachimento kara mita "*Amae*" [*"Amae" in Relation to Attachment*]. In T. Endo & R. Kobayashi (Eds.). *"Amae" to attachment-riron to rinsho ["Amae" and attachment:Theory and clinical practice]* (pp. 291–307). Tomishobo. [In Japanese]

Flores, P. J. (2004). *Addiction as an attachment disorder*. Jason Aronson Inc.

Fonagy, P., Gergely, G., Jurist, E., & Target, M. (2002). *Affect regulation, mentalization, and the development of the self*. Other Press.

Frydman, J. S., & Mayor, C. A. (2024). Scoping review on the use and potential of school-based drama therapy to enhance socio-emotional skills in early childhood. *Early Childhood Education Journal, 52*, 669–680. https://doi.org/10.1007/s10643-023-01471-1

Fujimori, K. (Ed.). (1999). *Kodomo no torauma to kokoro no kea [Child's trauma and mental care]*. Seishinshobo. [In Japanese]

Gersie, A. (Ed.). (1996). *Dramatic approaches to brief therapy*. Jessica Kingsley.

Global Gender Gap Report 2024. (2024). https://www.weforum.org/publications/global-gender-gap-report-2024/

Hartley, R. E., Frank, L. K., & Goldenson, R. M. (1952). *Understanding children's play*. Columbia University Press.

Hayashi, T. (2000). *Hayashi tatsuo serekushon 1 [Selected works of Tatsuo Hayashi 1]* Heibonnsha. [In Japanese]

Higashiyama, H. (1982). *Yugiryoho no sekai [The world of play therapy]*. Sogensha. [In Japanese]

Hiraki, N., & Kashiwagi, K. (Eds.). (2015). *Nihonno oyako: huan/ikarikara aratana kankeino sozoe. [Relations between parents and children in Japan: From anxiety and anger to creation of new relations]* Kanekoshobo. [In Japanese]

Honma, H. (2024, November 18). Violent and destructive acts inside and outside of schools—more than 100,000 cases. *Asahi Shimbun*, p. 19. [In Japanese]

Huizinga, J. (1964). *Homo ludens: A study of the play-element in culture*. Beason Press.

"Husband working same after birth of a child." (2024, April, 1). *Asahi Shimbun*, p. 17. [In Japanese]

Iacoboni, M. (2008). *Mirroring people: The science of empathy and how we connect with others*. Picador.

Inoue, K. (2013). *Gendai nihonno hahaoyakihan to jikoaidentiti [Mother norm and self-identity of modern Japan]*. Kazama shobo. [In Japanese]

Irwin, E. C., & Dwyer-Hall, H. (2021). Mentalization and drama therapy. *The Arts in Psychotherapy, 73*, 101767.

Ishii, K. (2023). *Kyoiku gyakutai: Kodomowo kowasu "kyoiku nesshin" na oyatachi. [Education maltreatment: "Education minded" parents destroy children]*. Hayakawa shobo. [In Japanese]

James, M., Forrester, A. M., & Kim, K. C. (2005). Developmental transformations in the treatment of sexually abused children. In C. Haen & A. M. Weber (Eds). *Clinical applications of drama therapy in child and adolescent treatment* (pp. 67–86). Taylor & Francis Group.

Jennings, S. (1994). *Dramatherapy with children and adolescents*. Routledge.

Jennings, S. (1996). Brief dramatherapy: The healing power of the here and now. In A. Gersie (Ed.), *Dramatic approaches to brief therapy* (pp. 201–215). Jessica Kingsley.

Jennings, S., Cattanach, A., Mitchell, S., Meldrum, B., & Chesner, A. (1994). *Handbook of dramatherapy*. Routledge

Johnson, D. R. (2000). Developmental transformations: Towards the body as presence. In P. Lewis & D. R. Johnson (Eds.). *Current approaches in drama therapy* (1st edition) (pp. 87–110). Charles C. Thomas.

Johnson, D. R. (2005). *Developmental Transformations: Text for Practitioners*. Unpublished.

Johnson, D. R. (2009). Developmental transformations: Towards the body as presence. In D. R. Johnson & R. Emunah (Eds.), *Current approaches in drama therapy* (2nd edition) (pp. 89–116). Charles C. Thomas.

Johnson, D. R., & Pitre, R. (2021). Developmental transformations. In D. R. Johnson & R. Emunah (Eds.). *Current approaches in drama therapy* (3rd edition) (pp. 123–161). Charles C. Thomas.

Johnson, D. R., & Sajnani, N. (2014) The role of drama therapy in trauma treatment. In N. Sajnani, & D. R. Johnson (Eds.). *Trauma-informed drama therapy: Transforming clinics, classrooms, and communities* (pp. 5–23). Springfield, IL: Charles C. Thomas.

Johnstone, K. (1979). *Impro: Improvisation and the theatre*. Routledge.

Jones, P. (1996). Time and dramatherapy. In A. Gersie (Ed.). *Dramatic approaches to brief therapy* (pp. 45–55). Jessica Kingsley.

Jones, P. (2007). *Drama as therapy-theory, practice and research* (2nd edition). Routledge.

Jung, C. G. (1968). Introduction to the religious and psychological problems of alchemy. In *Collected works of C. G. Jung, Vol. 12. Psychology and alchemy* (2nd edition). Princeton University Press.

Kashiwagi, K. (2015). Naze nihonno hahaoyani ikujihuanga tuyoi noka? [*Why Japanese mothers have strong child-rearing anxiety?*] In N. Hiraki & K. Kashiwagi (Eds.). (2015). *Nihonno oyako: huan/ikarikara aratana kankeino sozoe*. [*Relations between parents and children in Japan: From anxiety and anger to creation of new relations*] (pp. 64–83). Kanekoshobo. [In Japanese]

Kawai, H. (1976). *Bosei shakai nihon no byori* [*The pathology of Japan as a maternal society*]. Kodansha. [In Japanese]

Kawai, H. (1987). *Kodomo no uchu* [*The universe of children*]. Iwanamishoten. [In Japanese]

Kawano, Y. (2025, March 28). 20,320 suicides last year—second smallest for all ages but record high for elementary, junior and senior high school students. *Asahi Shimbun*, [In Japanese]. https://www.asahi.com/articles/AST3X04TXT3XUTFL02CM.html

Kimura, Y., Nasu, R., & Nishimura, K. (2020). Significance of mentalizing approach in group therapy for children: For development for children who have difficulty in attachment. *Japanese Journal of Group Psychotherapy, 36*(1), 95–104. [In Japanese]

Kittay, E. F. (1999). *Love's labor: Essays on women, equality, and dependency (Thinking Gender)*. Routledge.

Knill, P. J. (1999). Soul nourishment, or the intermodal language of imagination. In S. K. Levine, & E. G. Levine (Eds.). *Foundation of expressive arts therapy: Theoretical and clinical perspectives* (pp. 37–52). Jessica Kingsley.

Kobayashi, R. (2012). "*Amae*" kara mita Atachimento [*Attachment in Relation to "Amae"*]. In T. Endo & R. Kobayashi (Eds.). *"Amae" to atachimento: Theories and clinical practice*. [*"Amae" and attachment: Theory and clinical practice*] (pp. 17–31). Tomishobo. [In Japanese]

Kobayashi, R. (2019). *Boshikankei karamiru kodomo no seishinigaku: kankeiwo mirukotode rinshohga dokawaruka [Children's psychiatry from mother-child relations: How will the relations affect clinical treatment]*. Tomoshobo. [In Japanese]

Kujiraoka, S. (2012). *Episodokijutu wo yomu [Reading episode descriptions]*. Tokyo daigaku shuppankai. [In Japanese]

Kuroda, J. et al. (1976). *Boshi Kankei no Riron 1: Aichakukodo [Theory of mother-child relations: Attachment behavior]*. Iwasaki gakujutu shuppannsha. [Japanese Translation]

Landy, R. (1994). *Drama therapy: Concepts and practices* (2nd edition). Springfield, IL: Charles C. Thomas.

Landy, R. (1996). *Essays in drama therapy: The double life*. Jessica Kingsley Publishers.

Langer, S. K. (1953). *Feeling and form*. Scribner's.

Lassken, S. (2017). Persona non grata: A systematic review of de-roling in drama therapy. *Drama Therapy Review*, 3(2), 165–179. doi: 10.1386/dtr.3.2.165_1

Makino, K. et al. (Ed.). (2010). *Kokusai Hikakuni miru sekainokazoku to kosodate [Comparison of families and child rearing in the world]*. Mineruva shobo. [In Japanese]

McCaslin, N. (1984). *Creative drama in the classroom and beyond*. Longman.

McMahon, L. (2009). *The handbook of play therapy and therapeutic play*, Routledge.

McNiff, S. (2018) Philosophical and practical foundations of artistic inquiry: Creating paradigms, methods, and presentations based in art. In P. Leavy (Ed.). *Handbook of arts-based research* (pp. 22–36). The Guilford Press.

Mochizuki, N. (2000). *Jizobosatsu [Guardian Deity of Bodhisattva]*. Gakuseisha. [In Japanese]

Murase, K. (2009). *Kodomo to otonano kokorono kakehash: Shinriryoho no gensoku to katei [Mental bridge between child and adult: Principles and processes of psychotherapy]*. Kongoshuppan. [In Japanese]

Nakamura, Y. (1983). *Majo Randa ko: Engekitekichi toha nanika [Discourse on the Witch Randa: What is dramaturgical knowing?]*. Iwanamishoten. [In Japanese]

Nakayama, M. (2024, November 20). One out of three biased: Women for home and men for work. *Asahi Shimbun*, Evening paper, p. 4. [In Japanese]

Nash, E., & Haen, C. (2005). Healing through strength: A group approach to therapeutic enactment. In A. M. Weber & C. Haen (Eds.). *Clinical applications of drama therapy in child and adolescent treatment* (pp. 121–135). Brunner-Routledge.

Neumann, E. (1974). *The great mother: An analysis of the archetype*. Princeton / Bollingen Paperback.

Nihonmatsu, N., Yoshiyachi, K., Hagitsubo, M., & Okuno, M. (2018). Tsuyoi chichioya wo koseisuru tameno yumoa siyouni kansuru rironteki kenkyu: Kazokuryohoteki kantenkara [Theoretical research on the use of humor to constitute a strong father – From the viewpoint of family therapy]. *Contemporary Behavioral Science*, 34, 29–37. [In Japanese]

Nishimura, K. (2022). MBT riron no gaikan: imadokino kodomoto oya no tameno menntaraijinngu [Overview of theory: Mentalizing for current day children and parents]. In K. Nishimura. (Ed.). *Jissen kodomoto oyaheno mentalizing rinsho [Practice of mentalizing clinical treatment for children and parents]*. Iwasakigakujutu shuppansha (pp. 3–20). [In Japanese]

Noi, S. (2021). Characteristic health issues in Japanese children based on the "Concluding Observations" in the UN committee on the rights of the child: Focusing on the children's situation in the "competitive nature of society." *Annual Report of Japanese Association of Health and Education*, 28, 3–15. [In Japanese] https://doi.org/10.32314/educationalhealth.28.0_3

North *American Drama Therapy Association: Cultural Humility, Equity, and Diversity Committee* (CHDEC) (2021). https://www.nadta.org/cultural-humility-equity-diversity

Nukaga, M., & Fujita, Y. (2022). *Hatarakuhahaoya to kaisoka: Shigoto, kateiseikatsu, shokuji womeguru jirenma [Working mothers and their stratification: Dilemmas of work, family life and meals]*. Keiso Shobo. [In Japanese]

Ohinata, M. (1988). *Bosei no kennkyu [Study of maternity]*. Kawashimashobo. [In Japanese]

Okada, T. (2011). *Aichaku shogai [Attachment disorder]*. Kobunsha. [In Japanese]

Ono, K. (2011). *Iyashi to seichono hyogen a-to serapi [Expressive arts therapy]*. Iwasakigakujutu shuppansha. [In Japanese]

Onoe, A. (2006), *Kokoro hiraku drama therapy [Heart-liberating drama therapy]*. Kawadeshobo. [In Japanese]

Onoe, A. (2013). *Josei no izonsho heno drama therapy donyu to team renkeiga motarasu koka [On the effect on female addicts by drama therapy and its team cooperative practice between the caring and cared]*. In A. Mochizuki et al. (Eds.). *Taijinenjogaku no totatsuten [Reaching point of human service studies]* pp. 37–52. Koyo Shobo. [In Japanese]

Onoe, A. (2014), The healing and growth of little monsters hurt within: Drama therapy at a foster home in Japan. In N. Sajnani & D. J. Johnson (Eds.). *Trauma-informed drama therapy: Transforming clinics, classrooms, and communities* (pp. 329–347). Charles C. Thomas.

Onoe, A. (2024). The significance of mother-child improvisational drama in drama therapy for women with addictions. Fromnt the perspectives of attachment trauma and mentalizing. *Japanese Journal of Group Psychotherapy, 40*(2), 220–227. [In Japanese]

Owens, D. (2019). *Where the crawdads sing*. Corsair.

Pendzik, S. (2006). On dramatic reality and its therapeutic function in drama therapy. *The Arts in Psychotherapy, 33*, 271–280.

Pendzik, S. (2012). The 6-key model: An integrative assessment approach. In D. R. Johnson, S. Pendzik, & S. Snow (Eds.). *Assessment in drama therapy* (pp. 197–222). Charles C. Thomas.

Proust, M. (1983). Remembrance of things past 1. Penguin Books.

Ramachandran, V. S. (2000). Mirror neurons and imitation learning as the driving force behind "the great leap forward" in human evolution. *Edge*, 69. https://www.edge.org/3rd_culture/ramachandran/ramachandran_index.html

Rich, A. (1976). *Of woman born: Motherhood as experience and institution*. W. W. Norton Company.

Rickel, A. U., & Brown, R. T. (2007). *Attention-deficit/hyperactivity disorder in children and adults*. Hogrefe & Huber Publishers.

Rizzolatti, G., & Sinigaglia, C. (2006). *So quell che fai: Il cervello che agisce e i neuroni specchio*, Raffacello Cortina Editore.

Rogers, C. (1951); *Client-centered therapy: Its current practice, implications, and theory*. Houghton Mifflin.

Saito, A. (2022). *Haha toiu Jubaku musume toiu rogoku [Mother as spell, daughter as prison]*. Kodansha. [In Japanese]

Sato, S., Yoshino, A., & Shiina, K. (2008). "Bunshohyogen enshu" niokeru gakuseino mondaitento sono kaizennitsuite [Problems and improvements in students' "Text Expression Practice"]. *Gengo Bunkaron Shu*, 2, 129–131. [*Treatises on Linguistic Cultural Studies*: 2]. Chiba University: Linguistics and Education Center. [In Japanese]

Scheff, T. J. (1979). *Catharsis in healing, ritual, and drama*. iUniverse.com, Inc.
Shteynberg, G. (2015). Shared attention. *Perspectives on Psychological Science, 10*(5), 579–590. https://doi.org/10.1177/1745691615589104
Shteynberg, G., & Apfelbaum, E. P. (2013). The power of shared experience: Simultaneous observation with similar others facilitates social learning. *Social Psychological and Personality Science, 4*(6), 738–744. https://doi.org/10.1177/1948550613479807
Shteynberg, G., Hirsh, J. B., Bentley, R. A., & Garthoff, J. (2020). Shared worlds and shared minds: A theory of collective learning and a psychology of common knowledge. *Psychological Review, 127*(5), 918–931. https://doi.org/10.1037/rev0000200
Silverman, Y. (2020). *The story within*. Jessica Kingsley.
Slade, P. (1954). *Child drama*. Jessica Kingsley.
Slade, P. (1995). *Child play: Its importance for human development*. Jessica Kingsley.
Stanislavski, C. (1948). *An actor prepares*. Theatre Arts Books.
Tabuchi, S. (2022, November 7). When will all burden on wives stop? For couples both working. *Asahi Shimbun*, p. 23. [In Japanese]
Takahashi, A., & Yoda, M. (2024). *Hahaoyani natte kokai shiteruto ietanara: Katarihajimeta nihonno joseitachi [If only I can say I regret being a mother: Japanese women start telling]*. Shinchosha. [In Japanese]
Takahashi, K. (2016). *"Haha to Ko" toiu yamai [Illness called "Mother and child"]*. Chikuma Shobo. [In Japanese]
Takao, T. (2006). *Sokkyo engeki ha sozoseiwo sodateruka? [Impro education: Does improvisational theatre develop creativity?]*. Film Art Sha. [In Japanese]
Takeda, N. (2021). *Yarisugikyoiku: shohinnkasuru kodomotachi [Excessive education: Commercialized children]*. Popurasha. [In Japanese]
Takeuchi, T. (1999). *Ieru chikara [Healing power]*. Shobunsha. [In Japanese]
Tamura, T. (1996). Kazoku shisutemuto chichioya fuzai- futokojireinimiru kazokunai seiyakuwarino kochiku [Family system and the absence of father-construction of gender roles in family in cases of school refusal]. *The Journal of Child Study, 2*, June, 18–32.
Tanaka, K. (2004). *Boshi micchaku to ikuji shogai [Mother-child adhesion and childcare disorder]*. Kodansha. [In Japanese]
Tanaka, Y., & Ishida, T. (2022, October 27). Dad on paternity leave: Showing no responsibility. *Asahi Shimbun*, p. 28. [In Japanese]
Think Gender: Japan still has an issue of women discrimination abolition: Assessed and advised by UN Committee. (2024, October, 31). *Asahi Shimbun*, p. 2. [In Japanese]
Ueno, C. (2009). *The modern family in Japan: Its rise and fall*. Trans Pacific Press.
UNICEF: The State of the World's Children 2024 Statistical Compendium: Japan. (2025). https://data.unicef.org/country/jpn/
United Nations: Convention on the Rights of the Child. (2019). https://docstore.ohchr.org/SelfServices/FilesHandler.ashx?enc=ccYgnTYyhSecAf%2B5kwvpwdyXxQ7BzLDTR%2B%2FGZfFU%2FGQv3PeEP9EwmpL97yUBY1%2FrbaTbGrmz9EF6UcR0ruLFIA%3D%3D
van der Kolk, B. A. (2015). *The body keeps the score: Brain, mind, and body in the healing of trauma*. Penguin Books.
Way, B. (1998). *Development through drama*. Humanity Books.

Yamamoto, M. (2011). Hattatsushinrigakuno doko kara mita "Bosei Shakai" no yukue [Possible direction of "maternal society", seen from Studies of Developmental Psychology]. *The Annual Collection of Essays and Studies*, 58, 56–75. Faculty of Letters, Gakushuin University,

Yamatake, S. (2018). *Kokorono yamaini idonda chino kyojin—Morita Shouma, Doi Takeo, Kawai Hayao, Kimura Bin, Nakai Hisao [Intellectual giants who challenged mental disease: Morita Shouma, Doi Takeo, Kawai Hayao, Kimura Bin, Nakai Hisao]*. Chikuma Shobo. [In Japanese]

Index

For Product Safety Concerns and Information please contact our
EU representative GPSR@taylorandfrancis.com Taylor & Francis
Verlag GmbH, Kaufingerstraße 24, 80331 München, Germany